D0651657

Scraps of Wisdom From

# Grasshopper
# Junction

To order additional copies of *Scraps of Wisdom From Grasshopper Junction,* by Leslie Kay, call 1-800-765-6955.

Visit our website at www.rhpa.org for information on other Review and Herald products.

Scraps of Wisdom From

# Grasshopper Junction

Rediscover the Lost
Art of Being Content

Leslie Kay

REVIEW AND HERALD® PUBLISHING ASSOCIATION
HAGERSTOWN, MD 21740

Copyright © 1999 by
Review and Herald® Publishing Association
International copyright secured

The author assumes full responsibility for the accuracy of all facts and quotations as cited in this book.

Scripture quotations marked NASB are from the *New American Standard Bible,* © The Lockman Foundation 1960, 1962, 1963, 1968, 1971, 1972, 1973, 1975, 1977.

Texts credited to NIV are from the *Holy Bible, New International Version.* Copyright © 1973, 1978, 1984, International Bible Society. Used by permission of Zondervan Bible Publishers.

Bible texts credited to RSV are from the Revised Standard Version of the Bible, copyright © 1946, 1952, 1971, by the Division of Christian Education of the National Council of the Churches of Christ in the U.S.A. Used by permission.

Verses marked TLB are taken from *The Living Bible,* copyright © 1971 by Tyndale House Publishers, Wheaton, Ill. Used by permission.

This book was
Edited by Jeannette R. Johnson
Designed by Willie S. Duke
Electronic make-up by Shirley M. Bolivar
Cover art by Terry Crews
Typeset: 11/13 Usherwood Book

PRINTED IN U.S.A.

03 02 01 00 99          5 4 3 2 1

**R&H Cataloging Service**
Kay, Leslie Eileen, 1957-
       Scraps of wisdom from Grasshopper Junction:
rediscover the lost art of being content.

       1. Christian life. 2. Religious life. I. Title.
                       248.4

ISBN 0-8280-1348-9

To Don, the one I love,
whose help and encouragement
made this dream a reality.

And to Becky and Jenny, who
were (sort of) patient while
Mommy holed up interminably
with the computer.

# Acknowledgments

During the first year of our marriage, my husband and I attended a college week of prayer, where we were introduced to a message that changed our lives—the powerful, heart-humbling "1888 Message." We saw in this beautiful gospel presentation the true genius of Adventism: the practical Good News of grace much greater than our sin, showered upon us by a loving Saviour, Who came so much closer to us than we realized.

I am indebted to Pastor Robert J. Wieland for introducing us to this heart-warming, soul-stretching message that spring of 1986. I am indebted to his writings, as well as those of Jack Sequeira, A. T. Jones, E. J. Waggoner, and, of course, Ellen White. Though I have so often stumbled and become distracted in the intervening years, their writings have always been there, leading me forward into the arms of the One Who knows me so well and loves me so thoroughly.

It is my sincere prayer that the stories and concepts contained in this book have been true to the spirit of this most precious message of righteousness by faith in Christ, and that He alone has been glorified.

# Contents

# Preface

I realized just how far we'd moved into the country the first time UPS tried to deliver a package. Weeks passed, but no smiling man-in-brown came bearing the anticipated 25 pounds of Weimar granola. My husband, who is incorrigibly addicted to the stuff, began to exhibit signs of granola deprivation, and was soon in the throes of full-blown granola withdrawal. Finally, a trip to the Chloride post office produced a postcard from UPS, admitting defeat and instructing us to call an 800 number. I dialed accordingly and confirmed our address.

"So, you live in Chloride, Arizona?" the operator inquired.

"Well, not exactly. We live at a mine between Chloride and Grasshopper Junction."

"Oh, . . . and your street name is posted?" she asked hopefully.

"No, but we're really easy to find!" I answered brightly. I detected a discreet, but heavy sigh at the other end of the line.

"Could you please give me directions?" she asked, her weary voice tinged with dread.

"Sure! Just take Highway 93 north from Kingman, pass Santa Claus, and turn right at

Grasshopper Junction. Then, left at the big Silver Sage sign, stay on the dirt road until you get to the old rock house with round windows and no roof, and turn right. We're the gray doublewide by the big mine shaft—you can't miss us!"

The poor woman made polite, noncommittal noises, then I heard a click.

I regretted the pain I had caused her. I know how she felt. It took us a while to believe the Lord's plan for our family included the "gray doublewide by the big mine shaft"—a cavernous hole in the earth that could easily swallow a small fleet of granola-filled UPS trucks.

But here we are. And here is our story. It's a unique story of thieving coyotes, irritable rattlesnakes, and a surprisingly providential mining claim. And it's a common, age-old story of a family of believers seeking to know and do the will of God, struggling to make ends meet, sticking together by God's grace.

Most of all, it's a story of our wonderful, faithful Saviour, Who walks with us through all the large and small transactions of life; Who loves us, keeps us, and prepares us for His imminent return.

So if you ever find yourself cruising down Highway 93, somewhere between Kingman and dehydration, your reason and your radiator fast succumbing to the shimmering asphalt heat waves, take the turn-off at Grasshopper Junction. Stop at the gray doublewide by the big mine shaft. We'll give you a cool drink and a shady place to sit, and we'll listen to your story of how the Lord has led and blessed in your life.

And you don't even have to bring a bag of granola.

# CHAPTER 1

# The Tuckahoe

Our neighbor, Seth, was home watching TV one afternoon, when three young boys knocked on his door and said, "Sir, we need some advice."

Astonished that he had been selected for such a distinction, our friend cautiously responded, "What sort of advice do you need?"

"Well," one of the boys replied uncertainly, "advice on how to get a cow out of a mine shaft."

"I think you'd better show me the cow and the shaft," Seth decided, whereupon the three called their mothers, who (much to their relief) promptly ordered them home.

The boys were eager to go for good reason. Though they vehemently denied it, Seth had noticed them earlier in the day, laughing as they chased a cow across our property. As she fled, she stepped too close to one of our mine shafts. The treacherous ground gave way, dropping the cow 15 feet, where she landed with her front legs pinned beneath her. When Seth found her, she was bawling in pain and fear.

He phoned Billy, a local rancher, who soon came rattling down the dusty road in his pickup. Billy and his ranch hand lassoed the cow, and Seth tied her to his ancient bulldozer and pulled her up to solid ground. But her legs had been damaged, and she was unable to stand. After languishing for some days, she was put out of her misery.

It's a sad story, and we were sorry to hear it. If we had been here, we probably could have prevented the whole thing. But being here was the last thing on our minds. We were 300 miles away, at the opposite end of the state of Arizona, working ourselves to death to pay for a house we couldn't afford, propped up by credit cards we had vowed would never control us. All because we hadn't appreciated our inheritance.

It happed like this.

In 1989 my husband's father died, leaving him a spent silver mine. Located two miles west of Chloride, a decrepit northwest Arizona mining town, the "Tuckahoe" was 20 acres of open range and unfenced mine shafts. It became our private joke. Whenever one of us bemoaned the outrageous price of California real estate, the other would say, "Well, there's always the Tuckahoe. We could put up our tent and move right in!" We laughed it to scorn. We couldn't wait to unload it.

Not that we didn't want to live in the desert. Its arid climate had always been my haven from severe asthma and allergies. And it wasn't that we didn't want to live in the country. We had always rented in rural areas, always believed that "the Lord desires His people to move into the country, where they can settle on the land, and raise their own fruit and vegetables, and where their children can be brought in direct contact with the works of God in nature" (*Country Living,* p. 30).

But how could we grow fruit and vegetables in some of the most barren desert in North America? And how could we make a living in the middle of nowhere? So we dismissed our inheritance as a liability to be disposed of as soon as possible. We were ready to settle down, but not on the Tuckahoe.

In 1993 we left green, overpriced California for drier, more affordable Tucson, where Don had secured a job. We hoped to find a modest home in the city until we could afford some outlying acreage. But as I toured the beautiful new homes, I coveted one that was just beyond our means. And I got what I wanted. Within a year we were deeply in debt, and miserable in the city. Like the children of Israel who cried out in their Egyptian bondage, we cried out to the Lord to deliver us from our self-inflicted slavery of debt and discouragement. But even as we cried out, we cast about for our own salvation. Was it in multi-level marketing, in the sales position that would take us to Colorado, where Don would be away from home more often than not? But Don hated sales, and we didn't see each other enough as it was.

Our second summer in Tucson, I took the children to Arizona camp meeting, where I pestered the Lord incessantly with my two concerns—how to resolve our financial dilemma, and how to establish our family in the country. I shared my concerns with an old acquaintance in the Adventist Book Center, who responded with very wise words. "What do you and your husband already know how to do? What resources do you already have in your possession? The Holy Spirit will show you how to make use of them." [1]

This was the only sermon I was able to hear that camp meeting season, as I was otherwise detained in the cradle roll room with my daughter, Jenny. But I treasured that counsel and brought it home to my husband.

We wrestled with the concept all summer. What in the world did we already know, or have, that the Holy Spirit could show us how to use? Surely there must be something, but we couldn't see what. As we prayed and considered, we continued to dream of our elusive country estate. Don wanted 20 acres; I hardly dared hope for five. An elevation of 4,000 feet sounded perfect to both of us. And, of course, it would need to be in the desert.

That summer we found a buyer for the Tuckahoe. We just knew this was the answer to our prayers. But there was just one hitch—a minor discrepancy in the chain of title that was major enough to delay the sale. While we ironed out that irritating wrinkle, we finally surrendered ourselves to whatever the Lord might show us.

And what He showed us was shockingly, embarrassingly simple—the Tuckahoe. Our dreamed-of, prayed-for 20 acres of desert at exactly 4,000 feet elevation, completely debt-free, and already in our possession.

We stopped resisting. I quit whining about the dreaded mobile home. Don resigned himself to hauling water.[2] And somehow the insurmountable liabilities became assets. We speculated that perhaps the "creature from the black lagoon" didn't really lurk in the murky, stagnant goo at the bottom of the shaft. Just maybe the slimy, black stuff could be made potable. And the sprawling, sterile plateau of tailings[3] would make an ideal work area for Don's home business.

We bought a modest mobile, cried as we said goodbye to our first home, and packed our Ryder truck to the gills. While the mobile home was installed on the property, we stayed in a Kingman Motel 6, where we made a money-saving discovery. Situated as we were next to the railroad tracks, we didn't need to drop a quarter into the Vibra-bed.

The "magic fingers" were provided nightly, courtesy of Amtrak.

After four rollicking, thunderous nights, we trailed into our new home, a lonely gray double-wide, perched on a dusty patch of caliche[4]—with no electricity, water, gas, phone, or sewer.

"Was it really my idea to move in without utilities?" I muttered, as the harsh reality of our circumstances sunk in.

"It was your idea," my husband affirmed.

"And you went along with it? You're supposed to be the practical one!"

"I tried to talk you into renting until they could be connected, but you wanted to live on your own land."

So we bathed in our scant water heated on the Coleman stove, read by candlelight, and disposed of the contents of the porta-potty more frequently than the man at the camping supply store had promised would be necessary—and in six weeks we could flush and watch "Barney," just like regular people.

And now, two years later, we praise the Lord for our once-scorned inheritance—and the 65-year-old hitch in the title that prevented us from selling it while He opened our eyes to its value.

Our little piece of desert is rejoicing and beginning to "blossom as the rose" (Isa. 35:1). With some cultivation and careful use of water our dusty little patch of caliche has blessed us with tomatoes and squash, roses and marigolds, and the promise of more to come. Our children roam freely through the hills and washes, playing house under the scrub oaks, gathering wild flowers and juniper berries, their hands and eyes (and shoes and socks) filled with God's creation.

And we're still amazed that we really can make a living out here. Scrap metal recycling is not an easy business—or a glamorous one. But Don enjoys it, and the Lord is blessing his hard work. And we love having him home.

Our joy is tempered only by the knowledge that we almost lost this incredible inheritance. We almost sold it—because we couldn't see that it was God's provision for our need. In our careless estimation this stark, wild desert was a "dry and sterile ground. . . . In our eyes there was no attractiveness at all, nothing to make us want [it, and] we despised [it]" (Isa. 53:2, 3, TLB).

Strange blindness. Like the blindness that prevents us from seeing Jesus, our most precious eternal inheritance. The Saviour of all men has already freely given Himself to us, already eternally identified Himself with the human race (1 Tim. 4:10, NIV). But we don't recognize Him, because in our carnal estimation He has "no beauty or majesty to attract us to him, nothing in his appearance that we should desire him" (Isa. 53:2, NIV). So we seek for our salvation in all the wrong places, and labor to earn the love that God has already poured out on us from His cross.

We thank the Lord that He is not discouraged by our blindness. Just as He opened our eyes to the subtle beauty of our land, He patiently labors to open our understanding to the divine beauty of our Saviour, Who is "altogether lovely"—"a tender green shoot, sprouting from a root in dry and sterile ground . . . beautiful and glorious" (Song of Sol. 5;16; Isa. 53:2, TLB; Isa. 4:2, NIV). Because of His life-giving presence, our otherwise barren desert has become to us "like the garden of the Lord" (Isa. 51:3).

---

[1] Thank you, Linda Volkov!

[2] Not by bucketful—in a trailer-mounted fiberglass water tank.

[3] The refuse left after mining and milling.

[4] The crust of calcium carbonate that forms on the soil of arid regions.

# CHAPTER 2

# Flaky Jake

The summer after we "staked our claim" on the Tuckahoe, I began having a serious hankering for a dog. Purebred or mutt, I didn't care—so long as it wasn't a mincing little lap dog. I needed a hiking dog. A long-legged, intrepid companion to match strides with me on my daily retreats into the hills, by sun or moon, in snow or withering desert heat.

So Don and Becky set out for the county shelter to find The Dog—that noble canine embodiment of loyalty, enthusiasm and affection. They returned with a lazy, bone-headed moose, who coolly regarded us as so many fools to be bilked of an endless supply of dog chow. We named him Jake.

Don picked him above all the other pound puppies because, while they made fools of themselves barking and jumping around, Jake uttered not a woof, did not acknowledge his presence, and serenely went about the business of demolishing dinner. Here was a dog with purpose. My husband, a strong, silent type himself, appreciated such qualities in the future family dog.

We soon found that Jake's appetite was unquenchable and his palette utterly undiscriminating. He never met a disgusting smell he didn't embrace like a brother. Dog chow and cow pies were consumed with equal relish, with a shrubbery side salad and disposable diapers for dessert. Nutritive value, freshness, eye appeal were all suspect, and thoroughly avoided. If it was unfit for consumption, unattended, or slow, it was fair game for Jake's voracious jaws.

With such dietary dedication, Jake soon doubled, tripled, and quadrupled in size. But so much chewing and growing sapped every ounce of energy from his muscular frame. When not lumbering to his food dish or inhaling its contents, Jake lay in a catatonic heap of wrinkled brown fur, a single glazed eye surveying his domain with profound disinterest. We had to assume he was still breathing.

When Jake was about 4 months old and the size of a small water buffalo, I decided he was ready to be initiated into the joys of recreational hiking. Every afternoon I clipped a leash to his broad, sullen neck and lugged him, gagging and groaning in protest, across the road, through the wash, and down the rock-strewn back roads of the Mojave Desert.

When I had dragged him some distance, I would unfasten his leash and attempt to coax him on with praise and, when that failed, dire threats. But the instant my back was turned, Jake would hightail it home and hunker down under the picnic table. He simply couldn't grasp the concept of walking for fun. If it didn't lead to food, Jake wasn't going there.

As Jake's bulk increased, so did his loathing of physical exertion. But if he was doggedly determined to avoid exercise at all costs, I was more determined to see that he got it. He was *my* hiking dog and he was going to *hike*—and *like* it.

Fortunately for us, into the midst of this tug-of-war trotted an amiable Australian shepherd named Bo. Young, energetic, eager to please, Bo was the hiking dog of my dreams. When it was time to hit the trail, Bo needed no prodding. He lived to move. Catapulting through the gate at full speed, he didn't just run—he glided, he danced, he pranced. He sailed spectacularly over the desert scrub like a graceful gazelle bounding across the savannah. As I watched him easily cover 10 miles to my one, I knew I had at last found my canine soul mate.

I thought, *Surely Jake will see how much fun Bo is having and follow along in spite of himself.* But when Bo and I stepped through the gate with our faces pointed toward the hills, Jake resolutely planted his formidable bottom on the gravel and bid us a baleful goodbye. And he would not budge.

The unflattering voice of conviction began to steal through my stubborn resolve to win this ridiculous war. *Forget it,* the voice intoned. *The battle is over—and you didn't win.* This was a blow, but undeniable. Then what, I asked myself, should I do with the big lug? *Why not just be nice to him and leave him alone?* My authoritarian mind reeled at such heresy, but I had to admit that Plan A had failed. I decided to try Plan B.

I retired the hated leash and declared a truce. I went out of my way to pet Jake and praise him and offer him treats. At first he regarded these unfamiliar attentions with a cynical eye. But gradually he came to accept them. And as he saw that nothing was expected of him, he began to relax, and even appeared to enjoy the sight of me.

In time Jake accompanied us on our walks as far as the driveway, then to the edge of the road. And then one day the unthinkable happened. As Jake watched us cross the dirt road and descend into the wash, the faintest look of longing began to steal across his wrinkled face. The slightest tremor of excitement rippled through his powerful body. Almost imperceptibly, his well-anchored bottom lifted, paused, hovering in midair as he hesitated in the valley of decision. The struggle was fierce. I could almost hear the Olympic athlete perched on his right shoulder urging him, "Run, Jake, run! Cut loose, boy!" while the evil couch potato hovering over his left shoulder coaxed, "Relax, pal. Take it easy. Let's just sit back and think about this for a while."

At last the voice of the couch potato faded into oblivion, and the dormant Olympian leapt to life. "Go, boy, go!" it roared, as Jake cut loose from his anchor, ran free. Across the road he galloped. Into the wash he crashed. He thundered through the brush like a runaway Sherman tank. Catching up with Bo, he executed a pirouette of purest joy. Then off they danced, a curious but contented mismatch of flavor and style—Fred Astaire meets Arnold Schwarzeneggar, quiche meets Big Mac, butterfly meets buffalo. Bonding in a frenzy of body slams and flying tackles, their friendship was cemented. They had become buds.

As summer faded into fall, Jake became more of a family pet and less of an inanimate object. His surliness was replaced by an awkward but sweet affection. He showed signs of becoming a formidable watchdog. And sometimes he even came when he was called.

Then one day Bo and Jake found the gate open and disappeared into the desert to romp and explore. That afternoon Bo returned alone with an ugly gash on his left front leg. As I doctored the wound, I called and watched anxiously for Jake. But he never came. And he didn't come all that week as we walked and drove the back roads, whistling and calling—and praying.

Jake never returned. We speculated endlessly on the cause of his disappearance, especially in light of Bo's mysterious wound. Slow as he was, had he been overpowered by a roving pack of coyotes? Or perhaps been struck by a hunter's shot? The Lord only knew.

I dreamed one night that I saw him trotting up the road, a spring in his powerful step and a broad grin on his wrinkled muzzle. Coming home. Home to the family who loved him in spite of himself and his flaky, stubborn ways. Home to his buddy, Bo. Home to his beloved food dish.

We're so sorry to lose you, Jake. We'll always miss you, and the dog we could have watched you become.

# CHAPTER 3

# Only by Love

s new Adventists, newly married, my husband and I learned to look forward to Sabbath, our weekly mini-vacation with God and with each other. Surrounded by the beauty of the Sierra foothills, we loved to watch the sun sink behind the majestic pines on Friday evening, glad to exchange our six days of labor for God's gracious gift of Sabbath rest.

Such was our custom until the Lord brought us another Sabbath gift that completely confounded this restful arrangement. As darkness settled on our little studio apartment that Friday in September, I was obliged (despite my preferences and convictions) to labor on into the evening and all through the long, breathless night. And just as my advancing labor reached a crescendo of intensity that I felt sure would end my life, my agonized groans gave way to the shrill, insistent cries of Rebecca Eileen Kay, first child of her shamelessly awestruck parents.

My husband and I wept with joy as we held our little Sabbath miracle. We spoke in hushed, reverent tones, and gazed into her unfocused eyes until the morning light stole through the pines. As exhaustion overcame awe, I reluctantly surrendered Becky to the care of our midwives, and collapsed into my pillows for a much-needed, long-overdue season of Sabbath relaxation. Ah, sweet rest!

Never have I been so naive. Rest was not on Becky's birthday agenda, nor has it been on her schedule since. Our little dynamo leapt into the world with the flaming imperative of her destiny imprinted on every gene, emblazoned on every vocal cord. And that destiny did not include squandering her infancy on unproductive interludes of peace and quiet. Becky was born to be boss.

She bossed us early and often. She bossed us with missionary zeal. And she bossed us with volume. Every aspect of our lives, public and private, was overshadowed by our demanding, impatient, restless daughter.

The months of relentless volume battered my nervous system—and my fragile maternal confidence. I decided it was time for a mother-daughter chat. Facing my little interloper, I firmly apprised her of her proper place in the family hierarchy. "OK, honey, this is how it is. You're the kid. I'm the mom. That means I get to be the boss, and you have to do what I say."

Becky was signally unimpressed. She glared at me from her Johnny Jumper and brandished her blankie with the ferocity of an Amazon princess. And Mom got a vision of the tumultuous years to come.

Suffice it to say that for the past five years my daughter and I have clashed over everything from tapioca pudding to training pants. And in my efforts to bend her will to mine I have made more mistakes and behaved more absurdly than I care to publicly admit.

Somewhere along the way I realized that Becky and I had three options: I could brand her a hopeless incorrigible and relegate our relationship to the emotional ash heap; I could back off and let her run the place; or I could win from her that which I can never receive upon demand—her true devotion.

The only option I can embrace is the latter. It's the only one that works. It's the way God works with me. He is my Creator, and worthy of my allegiance; He is my Father, and entitled to my obedience. But I am an ungrateful creature; I am a wayward child. And I am reconciled to my heavenly Father only as I discern in Him my self-denying Redeemer. Only as I behold, by faith, "the Lamb of God, who takes away the sin of the world," can the "Spirit of adoption" awaken within my prodigal soul the cry of "Abba, Father!" (John 1:29, RSV; Rom. 8:15).

And so it is with my daughter. As her mother

and caregiver, I am "entitled" to her respectful obedience. I bore her in pain; I sacrifice for her daily. But her immaturity and self-absorption prevent her from appreciating such things.

So it is left to me to receive, in our behalf, the Spirit of repentance. It is left to me to confess our mutual rebelliousness. And then it is my privilege to disappear into the largeness of Christ's love, to submerge my will in His—that my daughter may behold, through me, His truly unconditional, self-forgetful *agape* love.

Because "only by love is love awakened" (*Desire of Ages,* p. 22). And it is Becky's love, not just her compliance, that I covet.

# CHAPTER 4

# What's in a Name?

$\mathcal{I}$f you spend any time in a grocery checkout line you've been assailed by the sensational headlines: "Aliens Invade White House!" "Incredible New Baloney Diet!" "Elvis Sighted in Bolivia!" That paragon of journalistic prevarication, the great American tabloid, wants to keep us informed.

My husband can do them one better—at least when it comes to Elvis sightings. When he was a kid, they weren't the feverish inventions that captive shoppers know and loathe today. They were a common, even daily, occurrence in North Hollywood, California.

My husband should know. He was there. He was Elvis.

His parents didn't know this in 1949, when they lovingly named their newborn son Eldon Wayne Kay. But when the age of the king of rock and roll arrived, his fate was sealed. His classmates couldn't resist, and Eldon became "Elvis the

31

Pelvis." And as such he was doomed to wander the corridors of Saticoy Elementary.

A decade later I suffered similar indignities as the fertile imaginations of my classmates at James Madison Elementary subverted Leslie Green-field variously into "Lester Greenjeans," "Lester Hayfield," and even "Leslie the Pestlie." I would have preferred "Elvis."

What's in a name? Apparently quite a bit—of dignity and identity, of heritage and expectation. We may or may not like the one we've been given. But we really object to getting stuck with one that doesn't belong to us.

I was baptized into the Seventh-day Adventist church on my twenty-fifth birthday. I liked our de-nominational name. It represented what I had come to love and believe in—the seventh day Sabbath, and the soon coming of my Lord.

But it wasn't long until I heard about our "other" name; our prophetic, symbolic, and (to me) prob-lematic name, "Laodicea." (See *Selected Messages,* vol. 1, p. 92.) My human nature recoiled from this name and all it represented—a last-day church that had been judged "wretched, pitiful, poor, blind and naked" in the eyes of its God (Rev. 3:17, NIV). Surely this was not a name that described *this* ar-dent new convert! It more aptly described my pew-warming, lukewarm brothers and sisters.

I am now 40 years old and am just beginning to

own up to my corporate name. I hear the "Faithful and True Witness" saying that my self-perception is inaccurate—that I am *not* spiritually "rich, increased with goods, and [in] need of nothing" (Rev. 3:14,17). And my perception must defer to the flawless discernment of the One Who "knows the secrets of the heart" (Ps. 44:21, NIV).

My "Wonderful Counselor" wants to lead me out of this pernicious, self-righteous spiritual denial, and into His complete, three-fold healing; a healing that will motivate and equip me to share the saving truth of a soon-coming Saviour.

For my wretched poverty of soul He will give His "gold purified by fire" (Rev. 3:18, TLB). The gold of "faith that works by love," purified from every vestige of self-interest—including the "fear of punishment, or the hope of everlasting reward"— at the foot of the cross, where the presence of my uplifted Saviour "is a consuming fire" to my sin (*Christ's Object Lessons,* p. 158; *Desire of Ages,* p. 480; Heb. 12:29, NIV; see *Thoughts From the Mount of Blessing,* p.62).

He will clothe my pitiful nakedness with His "white garments" (Rev. 3:18, RSV). In the garden, humanity exchanged the warm, protective care of its Creator for the chilly independence of self. And so we became helplessly exposed to the ravages of sin, from within and without.

My compassionate Saviour yearns to recover

me from this devastation, and restore me to wholeness. As I submit myself to Him, He will weave into my very being the heavenly fabric of "the garment of His righteousness," by uniting my heart with His heart, merging my will in His will, and captivating my thoughts, until His life becomes mine (see *Christ's Object Lessons,* p. 312).

And for my blindness He will apply the "eye salve of spiritual discernment" (*Selected Messages,* vol. 1, p. 358). As I become intimately acquainted with the Word of God, Jesus, the living Word, will open my eyes that I may distinguish truth from the devil's pretense. That I will see and abhor indwelling sin, disguised by a thousand rationalizations. That I can comprehend and cooperate with the redemptive working of God in a world of sin.

Laodicea. I may not like it, but it fits. Richly blessed with a knowledge of biblical principles. Poorly surrendered to the Spirit Who alone can animate these principles and make them a living, saving Truth.

I'm grateful that the God Who has told me the truth about my spiritual condition is also the Saviour Who, at infinite sacrifice to Himself, has "engraved [my name] on the palms of [His] hands" a new name that I receive in exchange for the old name: Overcomer (Isa. 49:16, NIV).

# CHAPTER 5

# The Language of Love

The Psalmist declares that out of the mouths of babes God has ordained praise (Ps. 8:2, NIV). By the time our first daughter had turned 2, Don and I knew from firsthand experience that out of the mouths of toddlers flow ceaseless torrents of unintelligible mutterings and gross mispronunciations.

But parents have short, sentimental memories. As the usual "kitty cats" and "bow-wows" dribbled from our second daughter's verbal faucet, Don and I waited eagerly for the real thing. For sentences, phrases—or at least English as a second language.

The wait is over. Primed by the hands of some mysterious inner clock, the faucet is suddenly gushing with verbiage, loud and unabated. Silence is forsaken, listening passé. Our soft-spoken sweetie has become an avid fan of the frequent filibuster.

Jenny has also developed an uncanny sense of toddler timing. Toddler instinct compels her to spring her most cryptic pronouncements on us when we are least capable of comprehending them. She approached me this morning while I was preparing breakfast.

"When Becky have birdie pottie?" she asked, peeking over the counter.

Preoccupied with a grill full of sizzling pancakes, I replied, "Sweetie, I don't know anything about Becky having a birdie pottie."

Jenny saw my difficulty and quavered, "Happy Birdie to you . . ."

I told her it would be this Sunday.

It's a well-documented fact that moms are incapable of conjuring a single, coherent thought after 6:00 p.m. We try, but the rigors of the day have turned our brain cells into grape jelly. We should be taken off duty promptly and replaced with fresh reinforcements of, say, an idle dad.

This is a fantasy, of course, so 6:01 found me standing at the sink washing dishes, my concentration impaired but my body still upright. Jenny sidled up and looked deeply and earnestly into my eyes. "Me hick," she said solemnly.

I sighed. Who could have introduced this innocent child to the evils of class-consciousness? True, we don't live in an upscale suburb, and our front yard is not exactly manicured. It's not even pedicured. It sports an ancient Caterpillar loader, rusting where it died six months ago, dirt dribbling from its lifeless bucket. And those Ford truck innards and bodies laying around in various stages of decay . . . My husband has promised me all this stuff is good for something. But does this make us hicks?

"Honey," I comforted, "always remember: you're not inferior to other children just because you live in the country. They're just being mean when they call you names."

"Me tummy hick," Jenny clarified.

One of these days I'll catch on. One of these days I'll realize that when Jenny says "Me want moonie," she's not threatening to run away and join the Unification Church—she just wants a smoothie. And when she asks me for her "hocks and hippers," she's not requesting an obscure Southern pork dish—she simply can't find her socks and slippers.

Baffled as I am by my daughter's creative incursions into the English language, I sometimes wonder if our awkward, lisping forays into the language of heaven sound like toddler talk to the Lord. If so, He is a more skilled Interpreter than even the most attentive mother. And He's never too preoccupied to give us His full attention. With divine empathy He "helps us in our weakness; for we do not know how to pray as we ought, but the Spirit himself intercedes for us with sighs too deep for words" (Rom. 8:26, RSV).

I am too seldom appreciative of this intercession.

Like a self-absorbed toddler, I'd rather hear myself talk than allow God to speak for me. Such self-dependence is not easily reduced to attentive silence.

A few years ago my husband and I became overwhelmed by the circumstances of our life. A new baby, a new job, a new home; too much debt, too little sleep, too little time with God and with each other. We had become very fragile. Don withdrew, and I grew lonely and bitter.

One night, after another interminable and fruitless "discussion," I collapsed into bed in an agony of sorrow. This marriage of nine years was disintegrating before our eyes, and no amount of words that human mind could conjure was putting it back together again.

I could only stare at the ceiling and whisper, "Oh, God, I don't even know what to ask for anymore—that You change Don, or change me . . . that You bring us back to our first love or take us through this to where You want us to be. You bring about what You know is best. Only let us fall into Your hands."

It wasn't eloquent, but I think it was language from a heart that was finally willing to listen to its Interpreter. Maybe I was ready, at last, for God's kindergarten course in the Language of Love.

Jenny's getting ready too. Tonight, as my husband and I deposited our little chatterbox into bed and kissed her goodnight, she reached out her soft arms and lisped, "Me hug and kiss Mama. Me wuv Mama."

No translation needed, honey. I happily submitted to her sweet embrace and left her room, overwhelmed with gratitude for the undeserved blessings of God.

# CHAPTER 6

# This Jewelry Thing

*I* found it no sacrifice to give up jewelry when I became a Seventh-day Adventist—not because I'm exceptionally noble and pure, but because I never cared for the stuff in the first place. The closest I ever came to being "bejeweled" in my pre-Christian days was when I proudly displayed the homemade leather bracelets I'd strung with beads purchased from the local "psych shop" (ex-hippies will relate to this). They never came off until they rotted off, and they went exceptionally well with my crazy-quilt-patched Levis and assorted rock-n-roll T-shirts.

So when I was baptized into a body of Christians who tended not to wear jewelry or excessive make-up, and dressed modestly and unpretentiously (this was in 1982), I felt right at home—except that I regretted having to part with my beloved Levis on Sabbath.

Imagine my surprise, then, as I watched my

new church wrestle over this jewelry issue, an issue I'd quickly considered a done deal. And imagine my greater surprise as I've since watched my two little girls, despite my example of profound disinterest, become magnetically attracted to the stuff. Though I've endeavored to inconspicuously veer them away from it and into what I consider more constructive pursuits, our oldest daughter, Becky, has caught on and asked, "Why don't you want us to wear jewelry, Mom?"

And so I've had to ask myself: Why don't I? Am I just a narrow-minded conservative, trying to clone my prejudices and preferences in my children? Is the issue even spiritually relevant, or is it a dead letter, a stale leftover from an uptight, obsolete Victorian era?

Now this is where I'd like to rudely interrupt myself and say that I find this whole jewelry thing surpassingly boring. Honestly, I'd rather clean out the chicken coop than even think about it. In light of the great truths of salvation, the gospel commission, and the imminent return of our Saviour, preoccupation with "to wear or not to wear" seems a tragic and self-indulgent distraction. But I owe it to my two little girls to consider my position carefully, prayerfully, and in the context of my understanding of the great controversy.

To do this I've gone back to the garden—the Garden of Eden. In that place where the spark of divinity was exchanged for the seed of alienation, in that moment when the beauty of holiness was traded for the disfigurement of self-deception, I find answers to all my questions about the mysterious workings of fallen human nature. In the garden I find the source of our universal compulsion to dress up, cover up, decorate, and otherwise reinvent ourselves. "The eyes of [Adam and Eve] were opened, and they realized they were naked; so they sewed fig leaves together and made coverings for themselves" (Gen. 3:7, NIV).

Self-motivated self-improvement is as old as sin. The naked soul blushes with shame at its exposed vulnerability and imperfection and seeks a thousand ways to hide. I've concluded that wearing jewelry is only one of those thousand ways human nature compulsively uses as it attempts to cover its nakedness and validate itself by asserting, "I'm attractive; I'm worthwhile; I'm a person of substance."

As I've said, it's not my style to "cover my nakedness" with jewelry or other material trappings. Because I'm reserved by nature and allergic to display, my attempts at self-concealment are more subtle. I prefer the comfortable cloak of intellectual pride and religious orthodoxy—they're not only harder to detect (and more affordable than a diamond ring or a BMW), they're harder to criticize.

But whatever our concealment of choice, we find the cure for our universal compulsion at the cross. There we find the One Who utterly immersed Himself in the shame of our nakedness—our spiritual nakedness and bankruptcy, as well as literal public exposure—that we might be wrapped in the warmth of His salvation. At the cross of Christ we find freedom from the compulsion to cover ourselves with any of a thousand contrivances; freedom to be clothed with the completeness of our Saviour's self-renouncing character—a character that is fresh and relevant in any age, any place, any culture.

So how do I explain all of this to two wiggly, giggly little girls? For now I try to help them see that their God-given, unaffected beauty can't be artificially improved upon. I try to tactfully direct their attention away from their appearance and toward the beauty of the natural world, the joy of service, the joy of learning and creating. I try to help them see that jewels are not something God means for them to *wear,* but something He means for them to *be—His* living, beloved jewels, gleaming with the eternal light of the indwelling Christ (Mal. 3:17).

So far, Becky's not convinced. She's told me flatly, "Just because you don't like jewelry, Mom, doesn't mean *I* don't like it—because *I* think it's pretty!"

All I can do is tell her candidly, "Honey, I know you're not like me. Jesus has made you different from me, and I appreciate that. But Jesus has also chosen me to be your mom. So I'll keep doing my best to lead you in the way I think is right, and I'll keep helping you make choices until you're grown up enough to make them by yourself."

And I'll keep praying that Jesus, the One altogether lovely, will become more real and beautiful to her than a thousand lifeless jewels (Song of Sol. 5:16). But should she grow up to choose the latter, I've let her know that I love her far too much to let it come between us.

# Forgive Us
# Our Debts

The photographer came on a bright, breezy
Friday to take our pictures. With the debut
of my column in five weeks, I was to appear
on the cover of the *Adventist Review,* an unaccustomed distinction for a housewife from obscure
Chloride, Arizona. Ever wary of the limelight, I reluctantly submitted to the camera, dragging my family—and even my dog—into the picture whenever
possible. But as the session came to a close, I was
surprised by an unfamiliar sensation—the faint, but
unmistakable, twinges of impending celebrity.

Sabbath morning my family and I departed on
the 25-mile trek to church. But not in the car. The
car was deader than a doornail, and had defied my
husband's best efforts to resurrect it. It reclined in
the sun, smug and inscrutable, as the four of us filed
past and stepped into Don's gritty 1972 Ford pickup.

Clattering down the highway, bouncing in our
Sabbath best among the wrenches and the welding

apparatus, I noticed the celebrity twinges becoming fainter. By the time we reached our windy, hilltop church and half-clambered, half-fell out of the great white beast, distinctly undignified and reeking of exhaust, I knew the video crew of "Lifestyles of the Rich and Famous" would not be visiting me anytime soon.

I can't say this was the Lord's way of nipping my overreaching ego in the bud, though it no doubt needed nipping. I can't say that because the real reason this all happened is a lot more mundane and closer to home. The truth is, our little wagon had been out of commission for a month—and we were still too broke to fix it. (And seven months and another break-down later, we still are.)

There's a reason we're so broke, a dirty little reason we don't enjoy admitting. It's called debt—massive credit-card debt—and it's been sucking the financial lifeblood from our family for the past couple years. And the funny part is we never thought it could happen to us.

For years Don and I resisted the urge to even own a credit card. But when we became convinced that it was to our financial benefit to establish a credit identity, we acquired our first department store cards, then graduated to the heavy hitters—major credit cards with ridiculously high credit limits.

At first it had been easy to honor our decision not to carry a monthly balance. Even after Becky's arrival, the loss of my income, and Jenny's birth we kept our commitment. But when we got in too deep with our first home, our commitment wavered and finally snapped.

With the bulk of our income swallowed up by taxes and mortgage payments, it had been so easy to rationalize, so easy to give in. *The kids need shoes; what can I do? Christmas already? Time to whip out the plastic.* I convinced myself that somehow it would all work out—Don's commissions would increase; our multi-level marketing business would take off; the Lord would provide.

Don saw the danger long before I did. At first I blamed his misgivings on a pessimistic, overly cautious nature, and berated him for his lack of faith. But over time even I could see the destruction that lay before us. That's when we decided to sell our home, buy the mobile and start a new life on our desert inheritance. Bad habits die hard, however, and I clung tenaciously to mine, stubbornly dragging them into our "new life." Though our debt didn't increase quite so breathtakingly as before, increase it did, inexorably.

Something—or someone—had to give, and it wasn't Don, who had remained true to his renewed commitment to reserve the plastic for real, dire emergencies. The problem lay with me. I didn't know (and didn't want to know) how to adjust my spending to our level of income. And though my patient husband never nagged me about it, the Lord, in His mercy, did—relentlessly. He spoke to me about it day and night until I couldn't stand it any longer, until I fled into the desert, desperate and ashamed, and broke down before Him in a sandy wash in the shade of a spreading scrub oak.

"I can't keep doing this," I told Him, "but I don't know how else to live anymore."

"Get rid of them," He replied. "Go home right now and cut up your cards. And don't use them anymore."

"But Lord!" I gasped, "How will we live? How will I buy the things we need? We don't have enough money!"

"You used to trust in Me," He said sadly. "Now you trust in your credit cards. Come back to Me and let *Me* take care of you. Let Me set you free from your bondage."

I couldn't argue with Him; I knew that my moment of truth had come. I trudged home and found my wallet. Firmly, I grabbed the scissors. Less firmly and confidently, I took hold of the worst offender and held it gingerly, even reverently, in my hand. Taking a deep breath, I prayed, "Help me, Lord," and positioned the card for execution.

But as I squeezed the scissors against the well-worn plastic, I was swept by an eerie feeling. It seemed as though the card had become a living, breathing thing, and I half expected that when I severed its account number from its expiration date, it would jolt off into eternity with a bloodcurdling scream.

I shuddered and dismissed the feeling as the product of an overactive imagination. Gathering my resolve, I snapped the card into neat halves that clattered mutely to the counter. The spell was broken. The remaining cards soon followed suit.

I wish I could say our fortunes improved after that, but they didn't. They got worse. And when we thought they could only get better, they got worse still. Those were dark days, when the bitterness of our debt bondage oppressed our spirits, and we understood the proverb, "The rich rules over the poor, and the borrower becomes the lender's slave" (Prov. 22:7, NASB).

But the Lord is merciful and faithful. By His grace, we clung to Him. When the bills piled up but the money didn't, we clung to Him as our Great Provider. When shoes and cars and patience wore out and broke down and the temptation to "charge it" was fierce, we clung to Him as our Deliverer. When discouragement threatened to overwhelm us, we clung desperately to Him as our Comforter and Saviour. And He always came through.

And as we clung to Him, we formulated a simple debt reduction plan that's served us well:

● We contacted our credit card companies and requested acceptance into their hardship programs, which resulted in significantly reduced interest rates and, in one case, zero interest. In exchange, our cards were "frozen," which was fine with us.

● We reserved one card for extreme emergencies and the occasional telephone order, with the stipulation that the balance be paid monthly.

● We realized that the bulk of our net income went to mortgage and groceries. By moving, we reduced our mortgage by $65,000, and our monthly payment by more than $500. And we discovered that beans and potatoes are really very versatile foods.

● If we can't afford it, we don't buy it. We pray about it. Period.

● We always put aside our tithe first, before we're tempted to spend it on something crazy, like the electric bill.

We realize that any lasting change of behavior always begins with, and is sustained by, deep, lasting repentance. So we continue to cling to the Lord as our only Sufficiency; as the One whose complete forgiveness comprehends not only the dismissal of our sin, but its total eradication from our lives. We look to Him to give us the strength and the resources to live with the consequences of our (mostly *my*), covetousness and unbelief, consequences that will surely require years to resolve.

And because I don't get out much lately, I have

lots of time to contemplate these consequences—especially when I glance out the window at our dismantled heap of a car, perched forlornly on blocks, its innards strewn ignominiously across a scrap of warped plywood. I try to remember how it used to look when it perched on four wheels and actually *moved*. I try to remember how respectable we felt the last time we drove it to church four months ago, how comfortable I felt the last time I drove it to the mall.

On second thought, some things are probably best forgotten.

# CHAPTER 8

# When Thelma Came Home Alone

Thelma is not your average barnyard bird. She is surely the most cosseted guinea hen in all of Arizona. No foraging for seeds or scavenging bugs for her. Our children lavish her with fresh celery in the morning, lettuce in the evening, and all the scratch she can scarf in between.

But Thelma's life has not always been so cushy. She started out as just another chick in the flock on Frank's farm. And when we brought her home with Beatrice, it was plain that Beatrice was boss. When Beatrice honked, Thelma jumped. And so it was not surprising that when Beatrice led the charge out of the confines of her new yard into the vast, cat-clawed, bug-filled desert beyond, Thelma followed. Beatrice had bigger flies to swallow, and Thelma went along for the ride.

My husband and I tried to shepherd them home that first night they strayed. As the sun set behind the brown hills, two usually sedate adults could be seen galloping and wheezing among the creosotes like a couple of asthmatic sheep dogs. But every time we managed to herd the birds to the edge of the road they had so willingly crossed that morning, they escaped us and fled back to the cover of the scrub oak, shrieking and chattering in panic. "Why didn't the guinea hens cross the road?" we asked ourselves. We couldn't figure. We left them to roost in the trees and face their fate for the night.

Beatrice and Thelma strutted home the next morning, proud and unrepentant, criticizing the food and disparaging their coop. Their wanderlust was not slaked. They plotted their next escape that night, and brazenly stalked out of the yard Sabbath morning. Their chatterings became more distant throughout the day, and they didn't return that night—or the next.

Our children were heartbroken and plaintively asked, "Will Beatrice and Thelma ever come back?" We couldn't say. Who knows what passes through the mind of a guinea hen (assuming it has one)?

When Wednesday arrived, we thought surely we would never see them again. But as we happened to glance out the window that afternoon we saw a lone figure shuffle into the yard, head drooping, her feet weakly making their way to the chicken pen. As she took a long, grateful drink and dragged her weary body into the coop, my children and I shouted for joy. Thelma had come home.

She hung up her walking shoes and settled in, passing her days patrolling the yard and bossing Rosie and Grandma, the resident banty chickens she decided had been placed into her capable care. Firmly ensconced on her throne, she reigned supreme as the Fowl Queen of Feathered Farm and was content.

Until now. Now she's in a snit because of Mary, Lucille, and Theresa, three new hens from her old home. Though they've been perfectly pleasant and courteous since they arrived, Thelma does not like them. She's convinced they are bad for the chicken yard. With head lowered and wings outstretched, she threatens them incessantly, forbidding them to socialize with Rosie and Grandma. Our once tranquil chicken yard is in an uproar, and poor Thelma is wearing herself out.

It's not a flattering admission, but this fickle bird reminds me of myself. Before I assumed my present identity as a mild-mannered wife and mother of two, I was also an incorrigible wanderer. When the mysteries of the Great Beyond beckoned, I followed, hitchhiking from one end of the country to the other, trifling with this job, sampling that regional culture.

Then the Lord caught me with His love, and I was baptized. I knew I had joined the heavenly host. With my rose-colored glasses perched securely on my nose, I became a zealous new member of the remnant church, an elite organization that does not eat meat, go to movies, or wear jewelry.

The glasses cracked over time, and I felt cheated—this church was made up of *people*. How had this escaped my scrutiny? I passed my days sighing and crying, casting wary eyes at my more "permissive" brothers and sisters. Until the pendulum swung and I had a falling-out with my legalism.

And then this astonishing revelation—everywhere I looked, I saw legalism! Why does this church refuse to accommodate me?

Praise God, He is longsuffering. He has not disowned me for my hardness of heart. He asks, "Do you think you are intrinsically better or different than your brothers and sisters? At your core, you are the same. You are born of a common flesh, woven from the same genetic material, capable of the same sins. Your pride is wearing you out—let it go."

He's right. I'm tired. Tired of playing church, tired of being an incompetent judge, tired of competing when I should be serving. But I can't just let my pitiful pride go at will. What I need is a revelation greater than any I have yet seen of the righteousness of Christ—a captivating vision of Christ on His cross. Then I'll live in peace with my brothers and sisters.

If guinea hens could comprehend such things I'd share this with Thelma. Maybe peace would return to the barnyard if she understood that she and Mary, Theresa and Lucille are sisters under the skin who all came here from the same place.

# CHAPTER 9

# Dedicated to the One I Love

*O*n the occasion of our twelfth wedding anniversary, I dedicate this chapter to my "Honey," the only man I've ever loved—my husband, Don. So if you have an aversion to sentimental journeys down memory lane, approach this chapter with caution—on a scale of one to 10, it rates an unabashed 11 on the mushometer.

Ours was a classic Adventist romance. We met when Don visited my church during a prophecy seminar. He was 34 and I was 27. I thought he had the sweetest smile I had ever seen. But he thought I was 18 years old—and would have nothing to do with me.

We met again six months later and became the target of a camp meeting conspiracy. We were "coincidentally" invited to the same potlucks and strategically seated side-by-side.* Sent out to hike Thumb Butte, we became hopelessly lost and wandered for hours. (By then, we didn't mind.)

One year later we spent our wonderful honeymoon at that same Arizona camp meeting. Don planned to enroll as a theology major that fall, and I envisioned myself the devoted wife of Pastor Eldon W. Kay. Instead, I found myself married to The Scrap Man of Chloride, Arizona.

A lot can happen in 12 years.

Mostly a lot that's been good. Like the two little tornadoes who blew into our lives, one five years ago, the other three years ago. Since their arrival, neither of us has heard a sermon in its entirety or completed a telephone conversation uninterrupted. The terms "date" and "disposable income" no longer hold meaning for us—though we've been told that we used to experience the former when we still had some of the latter. Even so, we're hopelessly in love with these expensive distractions, and with being a family.

Don was my strength that whole, long night of labor when our first daughter, Rebecca, was born. He never left my side. (He couldn't—his right hand was being crushed in my left one in an unrelenting death grip.) And I detected only the faintest whimper when I nearly yanked off his ear at the moment of truth.

And when our second daughter, Jennifer, made her dramatic entrance almost before the midwife did, Don calmly assured me, "Don't worry, Les. If Holly doesn't get here in time, I think I can handle this myself!" A brave offer I'm thankful he didn't need to make good on.

Besides being a great labor coach, Don is a man of many other talents. I'm continually amazed at his unique mechanical genius, his inexhaustible ability to build, repair, and assemble anything. And when I see those great, work-roughened hands that hammer and weld with ease tenderly bathing our two young daughters and gently carrying them to bed, my amazement turns to charmed admiration for this strong, gentle man.

And I'm still attracted to no one but him. Other men can keep their stuffy suits and ties. Don looks as great in a T-shirt and a pair of Levis as he did when I met him. He's the best friend I've ever had. We've worshipped together. Been broke together. Moved a gazillion times together. Settled our land together. After 12 years of marriage there is no one I'd rather spend my time with.

But it hasn't always been that way. It hasn't always seemed good, or even comprehensible. For instance, I used to think Don was a fairly chatty person until one day a few years into our marriage when I stopped "sharing" long enough to take a breath and realized how really *quiet* he was. Then the more I urged him to talk, the less he ventured to say! Talk about frustration!

And how could I have known I had sworn till death do us part to an incorrigible sleepwalker?

Who could have prepared me for the grueling, sleepless nights—the countless hours spent staring at the ceiling, silently clenching my teeth while my sweetheart ricocheted from midnight bear sightings to engine repairs to heroic rescues? Not to mention the unforgettable night I awoke, breathless, to find him furiously flapping at my head with a sheet. When I asked him what he thought he was doing, he peered dreamily through the dark and replied, "Putting out the fire."

It worked. Mine was extinguished for the night.

And even the rigors of childbirth could not prepare me for my greatest matrimonial labor of love—walking with this man on a journey of self-discovery that has taken him all the way from ministerial student to scrap metal recycler. A journey cluttered with the wreckage of the budding entrepreneur (including nearly every multi-level marketing plan that was ever invented), culminating in a yard cluttered with airplane carcasses, antique water meters, and miles of copper wire—the unglamorous, raw materials of a scrap business.

Anyway, you get the idea. A lot can happen during 12 years of marriage, a lot to wring the age-old question from the lips of the most devoted spouse: "Why *did* I marry this person?" I've asked it more than once, on my knees.

My answer has always been, of course, "Because I love him." But the passage of years has revealed the fatal flaw of my love—it's hopelessly dependent upon the lovability of its object. It's not generous enough to surmount even the common disappointments, misunderstandings, and inconveniences of married life. It cannot endure when called upon to deny itself.

As I began to see this I pleaded with God to give me *His* love, to love Don through me with *His* forgiving, longsuffering, everlasting love (Jer. 31:3). But even earnest, anguished prayer did not fill my heart with such love.

When I asked the Lord to show me why, it seemed as though He asked me, "How can you be filled with something you have not yet known? And how can you know what you have not yet truly seen?" He directed "the eyes of [my] understanding" to my crucified Saviour, because "the revelation of God's love to [humanity] centers in the cross" (Eph. 1:18; *Ministry of Healing,* p. 423). He urged me not to merely glance, as was my custom, but to intently "look on [Him], the one [I] have pierced, and . . . mourn for him as one mourns for an only child, and grieve bitterly for him" (Zech. 12:10, NIV).

I have found that when I take the time to look earnestly at my crucified Saviour, comprehending something of what it cost Him to die in my place, "a fountain [is] opened . . . to cleanse [me] from sin and impurity" (Zech. 13:1, NIV). A fountain that purifies the very springs of motivation with a cleansing stream of repentance and gratitude.

Such is the power of the cross. It's the only antidote for the otherwise irresistible power of self. I'm convinced that by no other means can I be motivated and enabled to love my husband with that divine devotion which alone can endure, whatever the cost, whoever he turns out to be—even if he turns out to be, in some ways, a stranger to my original matrimonial vision. Because of the power of God's love as revealed through the cross, I can honestly say I am content to live among the discarded pistons and water meters, sharing the lot of my soft-spoken, sleep-walking Scrap Man.

Happy Anniversary, honey! I love you!

---

* Thank you, Blanche and Colleen!

# CHAPTER 10

# Crazy for You

Most of the time I enjoy being a stay-at-home mom. Most of the time I'm content to clean up the house and work in the yard, all in the company of two busy little human beings whose thinking processes and energy levels defy the laws of logic and nature.

Most of the time I'm content. Even now, as I lay in bed, flanked by these busy two, who noisily insist that I open my yawning mouth wider so they can count the fascinating "shiny things" inside. I oblige, though I hope this isn't one of those defining memories they'll trot out in years to come. "You know that day we looked in Mom's mouth? Can you believe all those crowns and fillings?"

Shiny things accounted for, Becky announces to Jenny, for no apparent reason (none is needed), "Every time you talk, I'm gonna say 'Bo-Sho'!"

And every time Jenny opens her mouth, Bo-Sho it is. For the rest of the morning. Until Becky wanders into the kitchen and Bo-Sho is replaced by the five most terrifying words in a preschooler's vocabulary: "Can I help you, Mommy?"

Now, while I appreciate the sentiment, I've found that preparing lunch with a zealous 5-year-old is like trying to insert a contact lens during a hurricane. It's just not manageable. And it's not good for my aging nerves. While some purists might not approve of the tactic, I thank my daughter and politely redirect her to the living room to play Barbies with her sister. But I've barely returned to my bean soup when I hear, "Mom, Jenny spitted at me and she's taking off her underwear!"

Reflexively I call out, "Jenny, we don't spit." And to Becky, "Why is she taking off her underwear?"

"Because she's taking a pretend bath."

Sure enough, in the middle of the living room, my exuberant 3-year-old is vigorously and quite nakedly rolling around on the floor, generously splashing herself with pretend water. No harm done. It's a warm day—and a pretend bath is a lot easier to handle than five consecutive hours of Bo-Sho.

As stated previously, I enjoy being home with my kids. Most of the time. But I freely confess there are times when I most certainly do not. When the vile, loathsome specter of sibling rivalry rears its hideous head, I would rather be anywhere else (scouring the French fryer at Binky's Burger Barn, for instance, or hanging by my fingernails over a pit of writhing snakes).

Because these options are not available to me—by my own masochistic choice—I've learned the routine. I've learned that, as with any type of combat, sibling rivalry has its time-honored rules of engagement. Three come to mind: 1. Always choose the toy your opponent discarded six hours ago but will be unable to live without the moment she spots it in your tightly clenched fist; 2. Never ask your opponent's permission to eat from her plate or borrow her underwear until *after* the fact; and the ever popular, 3. Always reserve the loudest, most violent disagreements for when Mom is on the phone, preferably with the pastor.

In addition, I've observed that it is crucial to establish one's combat style early on to more effectively and consistently irritate one's opponent. While Jenny has always preferred "the tease" technique, Becky strongly favors "the boss." But they're unanimous in their hearty endorsement of the most venerated of all weapons in the sibling rivalry arsenal—"the tattle."

"Mom, you told Jenny to brush her teeth, but she's not—she's brushing her lips!"

"Mom, Becky thinks she's my mom, but she's not—and she can't make me mind!"

Even the dog is incriminated by "That mean dog, Bo, bumped his hard head on mine—on *purpose!*"

But for sheer torture and emotional incapacitation, every child knows that nothing can equal the effectiveness of The Whine. Nothing is more exquisitely calculated to reduce an otherwise healthy, well-adjusted adult to a whimpering, quivering pulp. The effect of The Whine on the auditory and nervous systems is much like having one's feet thrust into burning coals and one's fingers plugged into live electrical sockets, all to the frenzied accompaniment of a pack of shrieking panthers. Not a healthy experience nor a pretty sight.

So, it's not all great. Sometimes it's just plain crazy. Sometimes the whining and the tattling and the exhausting, irrational behavior make me almost feel like chucking the whole thing and running away to a convent. But (by the grace of God) I'm still here. And as crazy as my kids make me, I'm still crazy about them.

I'm crazy about their undiluted, God-given capacity for life. I'm crazy about their gift for transforming the most mundane chore into a celebration of the unexpected. And I'm so grateful for those truly transcendent moments when I'm granted a second chance at childhood through their expectant, wonder-filled eyes.

I feel the years fade away as I watch the fascination with which Jenny regards the smallest of the Lord's creatures. As she scoops a limp, gray moth into an empty margarine container, and admonishes, "Shhh, Mom . . . I don't think he's dead; he's just yazy and seeping." As she pokes and prods a stinkbug that has risen to the occasion and informs me its name is Julie Andrews.

I feel the fresh breeze of innumerable possibilities when Becky says with great seriousness, "Mom, sometime I'd like you to get a whale tank—you know, a fish tank, but with a whale in it, 'cause I really like whales." And when she proudly predicts, "The day I get my horse I bet I'll be a good galloper! I can tell by the way I ride my stick horse!"

And I can't help but go all warm and mushy inside when she confides, "When I grow up, I want to be a mommy just like you! I'm going to have four girls, and I'll name them Rosie, Rosalyn, Rosalee, and Rosemary."

When I ask "But what if you have boys?" her eyes roll heavenward. "I'm *not* having boys!" she huffs, even when I remind her that Rosie, her cute little chick, turned out to be Rosie the macho rooster.

I could remain under the spell of their enchanting innocence forever, but I know it will not endure. All too soon it will vanish, along with the stick horses and stink bugs, the pretend baths and whale tanks. As I watch my daughters reach toward the promise of maturity, I know that now is my time to treasure and celebrate their wondrous, one-of-a-kind childhood.

So every time I think of it—even when they make it hard—I tell them, and I show them, just how crazy I am about them. And I thank the Lord for the privilege.

# CHAPTER 11

# Delivered From Depression

Depression and I are old acquaintances. All my life, it seems, without my having willed it, without my comprehending why, depression has been irresistibly attracted to me. The attraction has not been mutual. Cultivating the intimate acquaintance of such unpleasant company is not my idea of a good time. But neither is it an easy matter to fend off the opportunistic overtures of this determined "friend."

It's not that I haven't tried. I've cleaned up my diet, try to get adequate rest, and regularly walk the soles off of perfectly good Nikes. I've confronted my painful past, focused on the positive, and gotten my mind off myself and sought to bless others. While all these disciplines and activities have greatly improved my mental and physical health, they have not slain the dragon.

When I talk about depression, I'm not primarily referring to the "normal" down times of life in a sinful world. I'm not talking about concern generated by financial hardship, illness or fatigue, or even heart-rending grief at the loss of a loved one. Such sorrow and concern can be traced to their concrete causes, and, when mixed with faith, can be soothed and tempered and prevented from spiraling into despondency.

When I say depression, I'm talking about the shadowy, amorphous heart of the beast, the root of spiritual and social alienation that resides deep within every fallen human heart. I'm talking about the subconscious source of Nietzsche's maddening "melancholia," Solomon's "vanity of vanities," Abram's "horror of great darkness" (Eccl. 1:2; Gen. 15:12). I'm talking about that universal, latent suspicion, not generated by any specific life event, but easily "confirmed" by so many, that there is no purpose, no point, no possibility of perfect love to cleanse and fill the aching void.

Skilled counseling, positive lifestyle choices, and human sympathy certainly have their place in assuaging this beast. But they can never eradicate despair because its roots are inextricably bound up with a painful spiritual reality that dates to the fall of our race.

When Adam and Eve severed themselves from the Source of all hope and goodness, they severed their posterity as well. They transmitted to us not the guilt of their sin, but its hereditary consequences—a fatal, fundamental flaw in our genetic make-up, an essential alienation from God and from our fellow human beings that is far more profound than the devil would have us realize. An alienation that is the essence of the second, eternal death.

Had not Christ, "the Lamb slain from the foundation of the world," interposed as our second Adam, that death would have instantly asserted itself and crushed out our race (Rev. 13:8). But because "Jesus tasted death for everyone in all the world," we live (Heb. 2:9, TLB). We live to embrace the reality and the implications of His victorious sacrifice, or we live to deny them.

Though I have chosen to embrace His sacrifice, I have been so slow to understand and believe all that it comprehends. I have been slow to see that when He stormed the gates of hell and slew the dragon in his lair, He didn't do so in the abstract. He stormed the gates of my most private, incomprehensible hell; He slew the dragon of despair and alienation in my fallen human flesh. He died the equivalent of my second, eternal death; a "death in which the sufferer sees not a ray of hope because he feels utterly forsaken by God, the horror-filled sense of utter despair, the unspeakable pain of divine condemnation beyond which [he] can expect no vindication, no resurrection, no light beyond a never-ending tunnel." *

On an otherwise pleasant evening some

months ago, for no apparent reason I received a visit from my old "friend," depression. And I cringed at its familiar greeting: *You're all alone in a senseless world; unloved and unlovable. It's always been that way; it always will be.*

For the first time, at my very core, I didn't believe it. For the first time, I saw clearly that on His cross my Lord bore away my squalid birthright of alienation and depression. On His cross He earned the right to place these words in my mouth: "Once I was alienated from God, an enemy in my mind. But *now* I have been reconciled by Christ's death. *Now* I have peace through his blood, shed on the cross." (See Col. 1:21, 20, NIV.)

Praise God, it's true! It's true for me. It's true for all.

---

\* Robert J. Wieland, *Grace on Trial* (Paris, Ohio: The 1888 Message Study Committee, 1988), p. 40.

# Love Lessons at Grasshopper Junction

Grasshopper Junction is not what it used to be. Which may be just as well, since Grasshopper Junction used to be a boot-scootin', rip-roaring bar. These days the weathered farmhouse in the back stands still and deserted. The eight-room flagstone motel has long been reduced to an empty, blackened shell by a careless cigarette. Even Jenny, the donkey, has gone to the place where cantankerous old donkeys go to rest from their labors. But every time we pass the old place on our way into town, I remember.

I remember the little potbellied stove's valiant attempts to produce warmth, and the winter wind that snatched it away and carried it out through the cracks in the farmhouse walls. I remember the smell of "regular or ethel?" as I pumped gas and sold "fool's gold" to the tourists who stopped at the rustic station. I remember the arthritic windmill and the water that was so hard it couldn't soften

72

beans, though you might boil them all day. I remember the cramped Greyhound bus that carried me, summers and holidays, to this remote roadside "oasis" to visit my father, its handsome, hardworking proprietor.

Grasshopper Junction, so-named for an infamous 1942 grasshopper migration, was an alien planet to a teenaged rock-and-roller from Anaheim, California. Perched on a desolate stretch of Highway 93 at the junction of the Chloride Road, it was a musty, motley collection of turquoise belt buckles, jackalope postcards, and Elvis paintings. Colorful locals with names like Squaw Tom and Squawk Burcham shuffled in to swap stories of days gone by, days I would never know. I found it fascinating.

Of course, the best part of Grasshopper Junction was Dad. A daddy's girl from birth, I was convinced that my father could do anything—shoot a pesky rattlesnake, build a corral for irascible Jenny, then coax her back home when she chewed her way out and fled down Highway 93, braying lustily as she went. He could take a splinter out of my finger before I knew it, cook sensational French toast, and tell the funniest stories I'd ever heard. And most of all, he was kind. I wanted to be just like him.

I thought I had my chance to do just that during my fourteenth summer, the summer of the Tote-goat. To my adventure-charged, adolescent mind, the old Tote-goat was a powerful black stallion, and the porch behind the bar the last frontier to be conquered. No matter that my sleek black "horse" was a lumbering yellow motorbike, and the steep hill to the porch expressly off-limits.

Dad had emphatically instructed, "Honey, you can ride the Tote-goat as much as you like—just be careful. And when you're finished, *don't* try to take it up the hill. Just leave it down here at the bottom, and I'll drive it up when I get a chance. Understand?"

Oh, I understood. I understood that Dad just wanted me to live to see my fifteenth birthday. I only wished Dad understood that even though I was a girl (and a skinny one at that), I could handle it. I could take the bike up the steep hill and park it coolly by the back door. If Dad could do it, I wanted to do it. I wanted him to be proud of me.

So one blistering August day, with nothing to do and no one to do it with, I cranked up the Tote-goat and thundered around the motel until I felt the tenants glaring at me through their gritty windows. Then, kicking the bike into high gear, I roared across the yard to the designated parking area. That's when I heard it.

I heard the porch calling me, challenging me: "Bet you can't conquer me!" This time I made the mistake of listening—and I determined to take The Hill. I twisted the throttle and screamed up the steep slope. But a terrible thing happened on my way to the porch—I panicked. Unable to wrench my frozen hand from the throttle, too frightened to turn right or left, I watched in helpless horror as the Tote's front tire lurched onto the cement pad, rammed into the back wall of the bar, and attempted to climb to the roof. Failing to scale the wall, the bike slammed onto its side, severing a fat electrical cord, and smashing half a dozen five-gallon water bottles into glass splinters. Still clinging desperately to my fallen stallion, unable to peel my hand from the vibrating throttle, I came to rest in a sea of shattered glass, which the still-screaming engine chewed up and noisily churned into powder.

Grasshopper Junction hadn't seen so much action all summer. The back door burst open, disgorging the day's catch of locals and tourists. Onto the glass-covered porch they streamed, turning my private humiliation into a painfully public one.

My father rushed to my side and turned off the engine. "Honey," he asked anxiously, "are you all right?"

That was the problem. If only I'd broken my leg or had blood gushing from a gaping wound—anything to justify all this commotion. But all I had to show for my ordeal was a faint scratch on my knuckle. "I—I'm OK," I managed to squeak.

Reassured, but still upset, Dad demanded, "What were you trying to do? I *told* you to let *me* bring the bike up here!" It was more of a plea than a scolding.

Speechless and trembling, I disentangled myself from the wreckage and stood with downcast eyes, wishing death would come quickly and mercifully.

Sensing my embarrassment, Dad put his arm around me and gently led me to the house, away from the terrible eyes. In the silence, I punished myself a thousand times. *Why did I do such a stupid thing? Why am I always such an idiot?* Not daring to look into my father's eyes, I sank onto the couch, burning with shame, awaiting my just sentence.

"Honey, what you did was wrong," Dad calmly reprimanded. "You disobeyed me. I told you not to bring the bike up the hill for a reason—it's too dangerous for you. Obviously, you realize that now."

Still unable to make eye contact, I whispered miserably, "I just wanted to do what you do. I wanted you to be proud of me."

Startled, Dad sat back and looked at the floor. Then, as the faintest smile stole across his face, he did something I didn't expect. He told me a story from *his* fourteenth summer, when he took a wild ride on a runaway freight car with the prized rifle his father had not permitted him to take—a classic story of 14-year-old foolishness and bravado, of near-tragedy and last-minute redemption. And instead of tearing away my last, tenuous shred of self-esteem, my father reassured me that he remembered the strange, convoluted workings of the adolescent mind.

Then he said deliberately, "Leslie, you don't have to do what I do to make me proud of you. I'm proud of you just as you are. And no matter what happens—no matter what you do—you'll always be my girl, and I'll always love you."

That summer I didn't intend to take (and fail) a "crash course" in motorcycle stunt riding. And I also didn't plan to take a crash course in unconditional love from a man who was not a Christian, but who had intuitively received from God a large-hearted love for his erring daughter; a love that would stand the test of trials far more severe and life-threatening than the Tote-goat episode.

Now I want to give something back to my father in appreciation for this great love he's given me. I pray that this man, who has worked so hard to earn everything he's ever owned, will come to understand that there is one thing he can never earn—the freely given, unconditional love of his heavenly Father. I pray that he'll hear *his* Father's voice reassuring him, "My son, no matter what happens—no matter what you do—you'll always be my child, and I'll always love you."

I pray that my father will accept this divine paternal love in all its fullness and allow it to transform him from a beloved but estranged son into a believing, eternal son of the living God.

# A Case of Unshaken Identity

I knew who I was when I woke up this morning. When I was jolted into the predawn darkness by a familiar pair of 3-year-old knees pressing into my vertebrae. When I was welcomed by the same sweet, unshaven face that has warmed me for the past 12 years. And when the 40-year-old blond in the water-spotted bathroom mirror peered sleepily back at me, that clinched it.

So when did the identity crisis set in?

During breakfast, when I asked, "Jenny, would you like peanut butter on your toast?"

"I not Denny," came the cryptic reply. "I Seesah."

"Seesah?" I repeated blankly.

"She means Theresa," explained Becky. "And I'm her mother."

"Oh. So who does that make me?"

"You're the aunt," Becky instructed. "We're visiting you, and you're making us breakfast. I'll have peanut butter and jelly, please."

Later, as I wiped off the counter, I was approached by my purse-toting 5-year-old. "I'd like to buy some stamps, please."

"Stamps?" (Why am I asking all the questions here? I'm supposed to have all the answers.)

Becky laid her pennies on the counter with a sigh. "You're Eva, the post office lady, and I need to buy some stamps," she patiently explained.

And so the plot thickened as my tender maternal ego was hustled from pillar to post office. When Eva was sent on vacation, her counter was commandeered by Rosemary. Rosemary soon tired of her new career and ditched it for a little house on the prairie. (And I didn't even get to be Ma.)

As my children blithely danced through their cast of characters, I admired their freedom and flexibility, their fearlessness—even eagerness—to be someone new. So unlike the apprehension and rigidity with which I've often responded to the Lord's invitations to grant me a new identity.

"I will give you a new heart and put a new spirit in you," He's eagerly promised (Eze. 36:26, NIV).

"But Lord," I've protested. "I'm not such a bad person. People seem to like me just the way I am."

"You will be called by a new name!" He's told me excitedly (Isa. 62:2, NIV).

"Actually, I'm kind of attached to the one I've got," I've demurred.

"Be made new in the attitude of your mind; . . .

put on the new self," He's pleaded (Eph. 4:23, NIV).

"But Lord, I'm comfortable with myself. It's who I am! I don't want a new identity!" I've stubbornly refused.

Thank the Lord He hasn't given up on me. He continues to plead and struggle with me through my stubbornness and fear. And since there is nothing new under the sun, I wonder if it all reminds Him of His struggle with another poor soul who was desperately in need of a new identity, but didn't know it (Eccl. 1:9, NIV).

The patriarch Jacob was also satisfied with himself and his self-sufficient ways. Though he desired spiritual blessings, he trusted himself to obtain them without the help of God—until the day the carnal identity he had nourished all his life fully asserted itself and amazed even him with its unexpected capacity for deception (Gen. 27:1-40). After deceiving his father and defrauding his brother, he was forced to flee far from his home, never to see his parents again.

Years later, alone in the desert darkness, crushed by the conviction that he and all he loved were about to be annihilated by his vengeful brother, Jacob loathed the sin that had brought it all about. He loathed the self he once loved and trusted. He longed for peace and cleansing, for the assurance that he had been forgiven, for a fresh, new identity in Christ.

All that long night Jacob wrestled with God. In the grip of a tireless Assailant, who apparently sought his life, he spent the best and the last of his strength and self-assurance. Wrapped in the womb of darkness and deepest repentance, he ebbed out his old life as "Jacob the Deceiver." And when the morning broke and found him clinging in utter submission to the One he now recognized as his Redeemer, Jacob was born again. No longer deceived and deceiving, he had received a new identity—Israel, "a prince with God;" for he had "struggled with God and with men and [had] overcome" (Gen. 32:28, NIV).

If my spiritual identity crisis does remind the Lord of Jacob's, then He is surely pressing upon me the necessity for the same radical spiritual transformation. And for this He offers no glib formula, no pat spiritual prescription. He presses upon my heart and mind the imperative of a repentance so profound and uncompromising that it uproots from the soul every vestige of self-sufficiency and unbelief. A repentance that, in the presence of His surpassing holiness, spontaneously mourns, "'Woe is me! For I am lost; for I am a [person] of unclean lips . . . for my eyes have seen the King, the Lord of hosts!'" (Isa. 6:5, RSV).

He assures me that from the ashes of such a veritable death will spring forth the new life of prevailing faith—faith that has the sanctified gall to grasp His mighty arms and say, "I will not let you go unless you bless me" (Gen. 32:26). Tucked away in the inner recesses of a soul that has become broken and apparently helpless, this faith is the vital core of a victorious new identity in Christ. An identity that can never again be deceived by the lie of human self-sufficiency; never again deceive to gain its unholy ends. An identity that remains intact and unshaken, though beat upon by all the large and small storms of life.

The more I see of my sinfulness, the more I long to receive this faith-animated identity in its fullness; to give up the struggle and rest in the grip of the only One who is worthy of my unconditional surrender. Yet I wrestle, sometimes in fear, sometimes in stubbornness, sometimes in ignorance. And I wrestle because it's my nature to do so. Nevertheless, the transformation continues, day by day. The old identity gradually gives way to the new. By His grace I'll keep holding onto Him holding onto me until the blessing is fully received and the transformation is complete.

# CHAPTER 14

# "That's Not a Bongo—It's Your Plate!"

Teaching table manners to preschoolers is an exercise in supply and demand like your economics professor never taught you—it demands more patience than any parent can naturally supply. Just when you think you've civilized the little Philistines, they surprise you with some unsavory new twist.

If smearing applesauce into her hair brought instant notoriety to Jenny last week, to what new heights could she take her celebrity with a liberal application of oatmeal with honey? Which inspires Becky with an educational insight: Did we know that peanut butter and jelly have similar adhesive properties, as illustrated by the colorful display on the roof of her mouth?

I realize that actual consumption of food is irrelevant to preschoolers. If any of the smeary stuff finds its way into their digestive tracts, it's a fortunate accident. These guys are into texture. I can appreciate this. But do they have to make so much noise in their pursuit of the ultimate squish?

Sandwiched between these two little boom boxes, I yearn for the good old days when my husband and I could actually hear each other conversing in complete sentences. "Honey, do you remember—" I begin wistfully, but am drowned out by the sharp drumming of Jenny's spoon against her toddler dish.

"Jenny, that's not a bongo—it's your plate!" I admonish, as the table rocks and rolls to the rhythmic knocking of Becky's knees on its underside.

"Girls, please! We are not practicing for the percussion section of the Phoenix Philharmonic. We're having breakfast!"

At last time draws its merciful curtain over another meal of infamy. I have survived this latest whirlwind encounter with my children's manners-in-the-making. And they have survived another encounter with mine.

Not that I smeared oatmeal in my hair or showed everybody what was on the roof of my mouth. But inside, whether my children recognize it or not, I am similarly immature and self-absorbed. Like them, I want the best seat at the table and the biggest piece of pie. And I don't always feel like being polite to the person sitting next to me.

None of this ever bothered me until I met my Saviour and saw something of His gracious, heavenly courtesy. In His presence I began to see my manners for what they were—a thin veneer of self-serving civility. And I didn't want to drag them into fellowship with Him.

So I embarked on a stringent self-improvement program. I prayed hard and read hard and sought to apply, by sheer force of will, the principles I found in the Bible and the Spirit of Prophecy. But even inspired principles of themselves were powerless to penetrate to the core of my soul and imbue me with the fragrant inner graces of my Lord. Beneath my new and improved exterior the same old me cried out for cleansing.

The Lord heard my cries and helped me to see that "Christ does not stand afar off and lay down right principles for us to follow; but He impresses Himself upon us, takes possession of us as we yield ourselves to Him, and makes manifest His life in our mortal flesh." [1]

I've been slow to learn it, but I'm so grateful to be learning it now. Christ's redemptive goal is not to make me a "better person," not to polish me into a well behaved heathen-at-heart. His passionate purpose is to restore in me the image of God. To impart to me His mind, His life, His divine nature through the Person of His Holy Spirit. And He teaches me that I receive His life, just as I first received His salvation—by beholding Him.

He invites me to "consider [Him] continually

and intelligently, just as He is,"[2] because "by be-holding the matchless love of Christ, [my] selfish heart will be melted and subdued" (*Christ's Object Lessons,* p. 394). Melted, subdued, surrendered—all the way to its self-centered, self-righteous core. And to surrender self, with all its well-mannered pretension, is to gain Christ, with His truly gracious manners of kindness, forgiveness, and patience.

I was recently given the opportunity to model these gracious manners to my daughter, Becky. The soul of perpetual motion, she rolled up to the breakfast table in characteristic windmill fashion. Neither of us knows the details, but somehow, with all that flailing, she became airborne, catapulted over her chair, and came to rest with her dish of soggy cereal dripping from her hair, onto her clothes, and into the carpet.

I missed my opportunity. I was not patient, and I was not kind. I fussed and fumed and didn't at all resemble my long-suffering Saviour. So a few days later, He kindly provided me with another opportunity.

Breakfast again. As my unfortunate daughter lifted her bowl of cereal from the counter, some sort of mysterious gravitational force again took hold, this time plastering the sodden mass on the kitchen floor.

As I rather agitatedly pondered the implications of all this *(Is the Bermuda Triangle located under my dining area, or what!),* I was reminded of another little girl who had a gift for spilling it, dropping it, and tripping over it. I was taken back to the Great Spaghetti Debacle, another falling food fiasco in two parts.

Part one happened on a summer evening on our patio. I was carrying a steaming plate of spaghetti out to the picnic table where my family was having dinner. But on the way to the table my spaghetti took an unscheduled detour. As I turned right, it hung a sharp left and fell to the cement with a resounding *splat!* that delighted my sisters for days.

Part two followed soon after. I was again carrying a plate of spaghetti, this time from the kitchen to the dining room. As my mother looked on in helpless horror, my pestiferous pasta slid from my speeding plate, quivered in mid-air for a breathless moment, then plummeted to its demise on the freshly cleaned carpet.

Chastened by the memory, I apologized to Becky for my impatience and returned to the foot of the cross for another desperately needed lesson on Christian courtesy.

When my daughter's soggy cereal finds its way to my floor that fateful third time, I want to be prepared. I want to be so filled with the fullness of my patient, merciful Saviour that my children can't help but behold His living presence in me.

Then we can become changed into His gracious image together.

[1] E. J. Waggoner, *The Glad Tidings* (Mountain View, Calif.: Pacific Press Pub. Assn., 1900; reprinted Harrisville, New Hampshire: MMI Press, 1972), p. 20.
[2] _____, *Christ and His Righteousness* (Oakland, Calif.: Pacific Press Pub. Assn., 1890; reprinted Riverside, Calif.: The Upward Way, 1988), p. 5.

# CHAPTER 15

# Is There a Veterinarian in the House?

When my husband and I married, we were your garden variety vegetarians. We ate our vegetables—drenched in cheese, on pizza whenever possible—and finished off our dinner with the daily adult requirement of vitamins and minerals found only in ice cream. Entombed as they were in saturated fat, our broccoli and zucchini barely recognized each other as they sped through our digestive systems.

Then we decided to go for the nutritional gusto. No more detours to Baskin Robbins, nix the visits to Twinkieville. We had become serious vegetarians. Snob vegetarians. The kind of obnoxious, elitist vegetarians who caused even Adventists to tremble when they invited us for Sabbath lunch. What to feed people who actually like scrambled tofu, and who rank sugar as a toxic substance, right up there with snake venom (and who feel it their solemn duty to tell you so)?

There is justice. We have received the recompense of the tedious. Witness the herd of expensive, gastronomical misfits that roam our yard.

Sam, our sleek black cat, is restricted to a pricey prescription diet for male cats with a history of urinary tract infections. But this does not prevent him from supplementing his diet with the heads of lizards and kangaroo rats whose misfortune it is to stray into his path.

Thelma, our resident guinea hen, thinks vinyl is a food group. The instant the door of her coop is opened in the morning, she gallops across the yard in her haste to unravel our patio carpet. She swallows each slippery green strand with rapt abandon, like Julia Child savoring a delectable new pasta.

And then there are the miscellaneous reptiles and amphibians that skulk and swim in our house. Spike, a locally captured horny toad, is hand-fed freshly caught flies and moths. But in spite of all that tender care, Spike readily hisses and lunges at the hand that feeds him. (We've warned our children that Spike is a short-termer.)

Percy and Sarah, the fire-bellied newts, care nothing for the convenient pinch of flakes we shower into the aquarium for their scaly compatriots. Gazing impassively through the glass, they wait in a motionless heap for their wriggling ration of live blood worms—which must be refrigerated and rinsed daily.

Well, what do animals know about nutrition, anyway? All they care about is taste. And real healthful living is so much more than food and drink. It has eight dimensions that encompass every aspect of life: pure air, sunlight, abstemiousness, rest, exercise, proper diet, the use of water, trust in divine power (*Ministry of Healing,* p. 127).

Our family has been so blessed by the knowledge of these eight natural remedies. It has made our lives more abundant on every level. Aches and pains have become the exception, rather than the rule. Previously incapacitating allergies are more tolerable, episodes of colds and flu less frequent. Our energy and stamina have increased. And best of all, our children seem to have escaped the asthma that plagued my childhood and adolescence.

We're learning that trust in divine power is not just a predictable bit of religious advice tacked to the end of the list. It provides the foundation for the other seven elements. To recognize the spiritual dimension of health at its most fundamental is to appreciate the reality that "to the death of Christ we owe even this earthly life. The bread we eat is the purchase of His broken body. The water we drink is bought by His spilled blood. Never one, saint or sinner, eats his daily food, but he is nourished by the body and the blood of Christ. The cross of Calvary is stamped on every loaf. It is reflected in every water spring" (*The Desire of Ages,* p. 660).

To think that the very food we consume comes to us at the expense of the life of Christ! Our breath, our thoughts, every physical and mental capacity we enjoy, is predicated on Christ's willingness to give up His breath, His thoughts, His very being for us for eternity. The realization has a subduing effect on the soul. Healthful living ceases to be an egotistical exercise and becomes our tribute of gratitude to our incredible Lord!

The Lord has strange ways of reminding me of this truth. Sometimes He allows my ego to get a good tweaking, as it did when I met up with my young friend Marie. Here's how she introduced me to the girl who accompanied her: "This is Leslie. She don't eat meat. All she eats is vegetables."

"Uh-uh," said the girl, who knew a preposterous statement when she heard one.

"I'm not lyin'! She don't eat hamburgers or anything! She only eats lettuce." Marie smiled sagely. "She's a veterinarian."

This was food for thought. Maybe I should consider a new career. With our menagerie, it just might help to pay the food bill.

# CHAPTER 16

# Viva la Difference!

Men and women are different. How did I arrive at this breathtaking conclusion? Very slowly. Painfully, pathetically slowly.

For much of my married life I've clung to the naive assumption that, except for our obvious physical dissimilarities, men and women are pretty much the same. I've assumed that we think pretty much the same way, feel pretty much the same, and want the same things from life. All I can say now is—not!

As I've struggled to come to terms with this vital issue, I've sought my husband's valuable insights. "Honey, I need a male perspective. How do you think men and women are different?"

His immediate and forceful response: "Oh, I *hate* these kinds of questions! I never know what to say!"

Which brings me to the most celebrated disparity between the sexes: communication. While there are always exceptions to the general rule, it's safe to say that men don't talk. They grunt, they mutter, they feign ignorance and amnesia, but they don't talk. A case in point: Sabbath mornings find my husband teaching adult Sabbath school, while I help entertain a small group of enthusiastic cradle rollers. Since I can count on my fingers the number of times I've participated in an adult class since the birth of our first child, I'm eager for news from the other side. I invariably ask on the way home, "So, honey, what did you talk about in class today?"

And my husband invariably replies, "Oh, you know—the lesson."

I persist. "Well, I mean, what did you talk about *specifically?* What did *you* say? What did *they* say?"

His mood becomes increasingly wary. "I just taught the lesson, and they made different comments."

By this time I'm hanging on doggedly, determined to glean one vicarious thrill from his morning's adult interaction. "Was the pastor in your class today? Did *he* have anything to say?"

But he slips through my fingers like Jell-O. "Oh," he sighs vaguely. "He was there . . . but I don't remember what he said. It's all sort of jumbled up together now."

And there you have it. I can say with confidence that we women, on the other hand, don't jumble it all up together. Women remember precisely what he said and what she said, what tone of voice each said it with, and how we felt when they said it. Yet our husbands inexplicably don't appreciate this devotion to detail.

"Did you call the mortgage company today, honey?" my husband asks when he steps in the door.

"Yeah," I reply, "and they kept me on hold for about 10 minutes while I was forced to listen to computer-generated light jazz until I thought I'd scream. Anyway, when I finally got through, I talked to a young guy named Rick, who was really courteous and pleasant, even sympathetic—although I had a hard time understanding him because of the kids . . . "

"Honey," he breaks in politely, with a careful smile. "Can you give me the *Reader's Digest* version?"

This has always baffled me. Why settle for the low-cal plate when you can have the whole, gooey enchilada? But I humor him. "Ten percent is the best they can do on used mobile homes."

So little, yet he's satisfied.

Communication style is just the tip of the iceberg, of course. It's just the outer expression of profound inner differences, physiological differences that are engraved in every cell of our beings, differences in what matter most to us and the manner in which we pursue it.

I'm no expert, but experience has taught me that while women are primarily relational and nurturing, men are motivated to provide and accomplish. Call it conquest, call it necessity, call it self-esteem through achievement, what men care about most is reaching the goal with as few interruptions as possible, and preferably none. When they do talk, it's not primarily to sort out their feelings. It's to further the goal—to gather information, to set up contacts, to zero in.

This intense focus on the goal gives men the tunnel vision that makes women crazy with frustration. It's what makes them forget (or remember, if they're lucky) two out of three items at the grocery store. It's what makes them oblivious to the thrashing junior is giving little brother right under their noses. It's what makes them oblivious to the "details"—and to their wives' feelings. Because women are generally capable of focusing on the goal while maintaining an unbroken peripheral awareness of our environment (especially the people in it) we find this apparent limitation baffling, if not maddening.

I've discovered that virtually every activity of a highly focused man's life is subservient to the all-important goal, including sleeping (resting up for tomorrow's battles) and eating (which is not so much engaged in for enjoyment, but to fuel the machine).

My husband illustrates perfectly this mealtime utilitarianism. Facing his heaping plate with the impassive resolve of a miner who must muck-out six cartloads of ore before the end of his shift, he purposefully grasps his fork. Choosing the peas, he plows methodically through until every pea is located and promptly dispatched. That done, he firmly rotates his plate clockwise to more easily address the next target—a steaming mound of mashed potatoes. And so it goes until every serving has been rotated and efficiently consumed. I once challenged him to eat counterclockwise, for the sake of variety. He laughed—but he's never tried it.

Of course there isn't a woman on the face of the earth who would practice this sort of gastronomical sacrilege. *We* understand how to blend each delectable bite with its harmonious counterpart, the better to savor the subtle nuances of taste and color—a dollop of cranberry sauce draped against a morsel of cornbread dressing; a bit of steamed spinach to add zest to the hearty but bland potatoes and gravy. And whenever possible, a bite of something intriguing from an inattentive family member's plate to complete the effect.

When we've finished, we've accomplished our goal no less than has our male counterpart. And we've also managed to enjoy the journey.

Of course, the moment you commit yourself to such generalizations (even for the sake of a good laugh), you invite a recital of exceptions. There will always be the talkative man and the taciturn woman, the oblivious woman and the attentive, aesthetically sensitive man. But variations of temperament and style can't disguise or deny the uniqueness of male and female identity, because it's a uniqueness established by divine design.

The Lord said to Eve, "Your desire will be for your husband" (Gen. 3:16, NIV). Like Eve, I've found that although I'm intrigued by a great many other things in life, my intense heart's desire is to know my husband and to be known by him at a level of deep, devoted intimacy, surpassing that of any other relationship. Naively, I thought this anticipated intimacy would naturally occur and deepen over time. When it didn't, I tried to "help" it along. Not quite understanding what I was doing, I manipulated Don with emotional crises and the fear of losing me. I begged him to "talk to me," then scared him away every time he tried with a never-ending torrent of words. I became increasingly controlling, treating him, not as the intelligent, capable man he is, but as a mere extension of myself, an avenue for meeting my emotional needs.

Don has found that the Lord knew what He was talking about when He told Adam "through painful toil . . . [and] the sweat of your brow you will eat your food" (Gen. 3:17, 19, NIV). Though it exhausts and often frustrates him, his work has been his life and his primary source of self-esteem. Absorbed in it by choice and by perceived necessity, he's often lived among us as a stranger. Irritated and puzzled by the intensity of my frustration with his emotional distance and nonparticipation, he's found escape and solace—where else?—at work.

The wounds inflicted by years of this sort of working at cross purposes have caused us both a great deal of pain. Untreated, they festered into bitter hostility and alienation. And without our understanding exactly how or why, they brought a slow, lingering death to our once-thriving relationship.

Don and I are practical, determined people. So, discouraged but not defeated, we resolved to resurrect our lifeless marriage. In keeping with conventional wisdom, we worked on our attitudes and communication skills. We regarded our disagreements as "challenges" and "opportunities for growth" instead of grounds for divorce. We learned to carefully say "I feel" instead of rashly accusing "you always." But we mistook the symptoms for the illness, and the tools and techniques for the cure. Piled on top of our not thoroughly converted hearts and minds, such techniques merely compounded our problem by making me a more sophisticated manipulator and Don a more skilled and determined evader.

The conviction came to us slowly that because our uniqueness penetrates to the depths of our divinely-created, sin-damaged souls, we needed more than behavior modification. We needed a Saviour. We needed the unfettered, indwelling presence of One Who brings complete healing and reconciliation. And for that to happen, we needed to see ourselves and all our vain attempts to "fix" ourselves and each other crucified with Christ, because the living plant of reconciliation can take root only in the broken soil of a repentant heart.

Broken we became, helpless and disillusioned with ourselves. The process was agonizingly painful (and is far from complete). But it made us willing and able to see that although all the resourcefulness and passion of "human decision or [human] will" could not resurrect our dead marriage, a new one *could* be "born of God" (John 1:13, NIV). Wounded, disparate, and sinful as we were, we *could* be fused into "one flesh" and "one mind" through the ministry of reconciliation effected at the cross (Gen. 2:24; Phil. 2:2).

"For [Christ] himself is our peace, who has made the two one and has destroyed the barrier, the dividing wall of hostility. . . . His purpose was to create in himself one new [person] out of the two, thus making peace, and in this one body to reconcile both of them to God through the cross, by which he put to death their hostility" (Eph. 2:14-16, NIV).

Our dividing wall of hostility was built on the foundation of our ignorance and self-centeredness. It was reinforced by years of misunderstandings and striving for the mastery, fortified by many well-meant but counterproductive carnal attempts to break it down. It was destroyed at the cross, where the message of reconciliation was proclaimed: "There is neither Jew nor Greek, slave nor free, male nor female; for [we] are all one in Christ Jesus" (Gal. 3:28, NIV).

The Lord has been true to His Word. As we believe the message of the cross and by faith participate in its ministry of reconciliation, our differences no longer calcify into walls of alienation and hostility. Though the mysterious inner workings of my husband's mind continue to baffle and amaze me (he assures me this works both ways), in Christ I can graciously accept and respect that which I don't understand.

And acceptance is just the beginning. In Christ we're learning to build a new and living structure on this foundation of sanctified acceptance—no longer a wall of hostility, but a sanctuary of reconciliation. A place of peace where, surrendered to Christ and daily instructed by His Word and His Spirit, we can be cleansed, enlightened and enriched. Cleansed of the self-centeredness that creates division. Enlightened that we may discern how we've ignorantly offended and devalued. Enriched and complemented by the unique contributions each of us makes to our union.

I can honestly say that, to my knowledge, I no longer try to emotionally bully and manipulate my husband—not because I try very hard not to, but because I've lost the desire. I've become convinced that it's dishonest and demeaning (to both of us), and it doesn't work. I'm learning to present my concerns simply and honestly, and to then pray and wait respectfully for my husband to respond. And (most excruciating of all) as long as the ball remains in his court, I leave it there until *he* does something with it.

The Lord is helping me to see Don through new eyes, eyes that can discern and appreciate his unique, valuable qualities and insights. I'm beginning to understand that his "tunnel vision" is precisely what makes him a good provider. It enables him to slog through the discomfort of bitter cold and blazing heat, of mud, grease, and just plain hard, exhausting work to make his family comfortable and secure. And when my permeable, diffuse world wears me out, I know I'll find solace and a renewed sense of perspective in the center of his calm, focused universe.

I know Don will never be the communicator of my dreams. I realize that in a whole week he'll probably never match the volume of verbiage that proceeds from my mouth on any given day. But I know that when he *does* open up, he always has something worthwhile to say. And by God's grace I want to be there *listening*.

I'm learning once again to love my husband, not from an aching, inner emptiness, but from the overflowing fullness of my indwelling Saviour. I'm learning to appreciate his earnest, thoughtful efforts at intimacy and family involvement. In more ways than I can explain, my union with this unique, mysterious man brings purpose and completeness to my life.

I think Don feels the same way toward me. But I didn't want to make any assumptions, so I asked him, "Honey, do you think it's true that 'a wife softens and improves her husband's character and gives it completeness'?" (*Adventist Home,* p. 99).

"Absolutely! No doubt in my mind!" he gushed from behind his Sabbath school lesson.

Surprised by his unexpected enthusiasm, I pressed, "So you appreciate that about women?"

"Oh, positively! Incredibly so!" he gushed again, a bit distractedly, his eyes still riveted on his quarterly.

I smelled an evasion tactic. "A little heavy on the gushy adverbs and light on the specifics," I said dryly. "Can you elaborate?"

"Oh, I *hate* these conversations," he groaned desperately. "I never know what to say."

"Maybe it would help if I ask the question another way," I offered. "What *don't* you appreciate about women?"

Looking me straight in the eye for the first time since dinner, he solemnly intoned, "They ask too many questions."

So there you have it, straight from the horse's—or rather, husband's—reluctant mouth. Different is good. Opposites can complement. The battle of the sexes *can* be settled peacefully and amicably, through the ministry of reconciliation effected at the cross—as long as the combatants don't ruin the whole thing by asking too many tiresome questions.

# CHAPTER 17

# Camp Meeting or Bust!

e've plucked the last zucchini from the garden, stolen the last egg from our squawking hens, and kissed the cat good-bye. From the back seat, our daughters try to console our sullen dogs, who watch morosely as their world rolls away in an overloaded brown Nissan.

We can't afford it—and we don't really have the time—but we're on the road to camp meeting.

To the endless refrain of "Jenny's looking at me!" and "Becky took my Barbie!" the dusty, desert towns of old Route 66 roll by. Hackberry, where you can still buy a 40 acre "ranch" for only $495 an acre. Peach Springs, where the infernal desert wind nearly sends the kids' plastic picnic table sailing off the ski rack. Seligman, where the sight of the "Roadkill Steakhouse" helps us remember why we're vegetarians.

From Ashfork we travel south through the juniper trees to the pine covered mountains of

105

Prescott, Arizona. When we arrive a couple hours before Sabbath, we feel like we've come home. Thank the Lord for camp meeting! An inexpensive country vacation, at its least. An opportunity for personal and corporate spiritual renewal, at its best. Beyond the ever-present dust that falls like ash from Mount St. Helens, beyond the gargantuan spiders (or "pizers," as 3-year-old Jenny shrieks whenever she encounters one in the bathroom), beyond the rickety bunk beds and cockeyed showerheads, I find my brothers and sisters in Christ. And as the Holy Spirit refreshes my soul, He binds my heart to theirs.

Ed and Anita from Albuquerque, for instance, just down the hill from us. They're not sure how He did it, but last year the Lord enabled them to put a young man from New York's inner city through Thunderbird Adventist Academy—an expense not anticipated in their budget.

And Erwin, two cabins down. Nine years ago Erwin's walk with the Lord was sidetracked by an independent ministry with a critical spirit and a penchant for preaching fear. Disillusioned with the church and terrified of impending economic collapse, Erwin fled to the South American rain forest. But Erwin's haven became his prison. Armed robbers, thieving caretakers, and his faltering farm emotionally and financially drained him. Last spring he prayed in desperation, "Oh, God, show me where to make my home, even if it takes another armed robbery." Five minutes later, Erwin was robbed at gunpoint on his way home from the bank. He returned to Arizona with a new compassion for human frailty and an intense desire to discover his ministry for Christ.

Rollie, from Yuma, is discovering his ministry. Although Roy Adams, associate editor for the *Adventist Review,* doesn't know it, he's responsible for my acquaintance with Rollie. Embarrassing details follow:

The night after I met Adams, he spotted me in the audience and invited me up to the platform. As he graciously introduced the *"Adventist Review*'s newest columnist," I'm sure he didn't realize the speed with which this columnist was succumbing to a paralyzing case of stage fright. I smiled and faked it until he turned the microphone over to me with a blithe "And what can you tell these people about the *Review?*"

Review? *Did I know anything about the* Review? *Anything coherent?* As I glanced dumbly from the malevolent microphone to the expectant faces before me, my legs took on the consistency of warm Jell-O, and my throat withered into a vast Sahara.. To loosely paraphrase Revelation 6:14, my mind departed like a scroll when it is rolled up, and every rational thought was removed from its place. A few disjointed syllables escaped my wobbly tongue, but it was no use. I was history. My surging adrenaline had absconded with my wits. I quietly confessed, "Really, I'm a writer, not a speaker." Adams mercifully hustled me off to my seat. (After the service, every grandmother in the audience came forward to console me—"I know just how you feel, dear. It always happens to me too.")

The next day as I was grazing at the vegemeat sample table, the words "So you're a writer, not a speaker?" wafted to me on a breeze heavy with the scent of sautéing Chik Nuggets. I winced and peered behind the green post to my right from whence the voice came. That's when I met Rollie, its bearded, cherubic owner.

Rollie coleads in the primary division and organizes vespers at his church in Yuma. His burning desire is to gather the children in his care to Christ, and to gather his church family together in joyful worship and meaningful fellowship. His enthusiasm refreshed me. Even so, I fervently wished I'd be spared any more reminders of my recent humiliation. But it was not to be. On the contrary, it had become my defining camp meeting moment.

That evening at the snack bar, as I tried to disappear behind my husband's haystack, a gentleman approached me. "Are you the writer?"

Escape was impossible. I nodded my head grimly. "That's right—the writer, not the speaker." I might as well accept it—I would carry those words

to my grave. When I take flight on resurrection
morn, I just know I'll glance back at the epitaph on
my tombstone:

When Brother Adams called her nigh,
Her wits conspired to leave her.
She verily did sigh, and cry,
"I'm a writer, not a speaker!"

And so it went until Sunday morning, when it
came time to ponder that age-old camp meeting
mystery, "How come all the stuff that came *out* of
the car never fits back *into* it?" Time to dispose of
the bowl of red ants Jenny has spent the morning
collecting. Time to say goodbye for another year.

With our transmission ailing severely, we pray
our way back through the juniper-clad hills. At
Seligman, we exit streamlined Interstate 40 in
favor of less direct but friendlier Route 66. Our kids
nap as the sleepy towns slip by. In the unaccustomed quiet, it occurs to me that my moment of
public vulnerability was the means of my introduc-
tion to so many brothers and sisters I would not
otherwise have met. And I count it all a blessing because, like Rollie, I'm a gatherer. I gather these precious people and their stories into my heart.

There's Orvella, the poet, who lives an hour's
drive down a dirt road in the tiny mountain town
of Crown King. Karen, the teacher from Holbrook
Indian School, and the man who asked, "Did you
really jump up and down and scream and cry when

the *Adventist Review* called to say you were a columnist?" (Yes, I did—after I hung up the phone.)

I praise the Lord for the pleasure of meeting them, for the privilege of praying for them throughout the year, for the privilege of writing (as opposed to speaking), about them. They are my camp meeting gift of grace.

They're the reason my family and I will kiss the cat goodbye and hit that long, hot road to camp meeting again next year.

# CHAPTER 18

# From the Children of God to the Bride of Christ

**K**en and Barbie have been making feverish preparations. They've had no time to cruise the beach in Barbie's aqua-blue Jeep. No time for parties on the patio under the pink umbrella. No time for distractions. Ever since Barbie got her gorgeous new bridal gown, matching veil, and dainty white pumps, one thought has reigned supreme in her otherwise air-filled blond head—the wedding.

She dreams of it day and night. She thinks of nothing else—how she'll turn heads when she floats down the aisle like a vision of gossamer and silk. How she and her prince will trot off into the pastel sunset astride White Cloud, her flawlessly coiffed white horse. How . . .

"How do people fall in love?" Six-year-old Becky breaks from her romantic reverie and looks purposefully into my eyes.

"Well," I venture, "they don't really *fall* in love.

111

They start out liking each other, and the better they get to know each other, the more they *grow* into love." A solid answer, but sorely lacking in the stuff of legendary romance.

Becky looks unimpressed, as she does with all of my answers, and settles down to give the matter serious thought. After some deliberation, she asks, "Why do people get married?"

"First, they think and pray a lot about it. Then they talk it over with their parents," I add, studying her face to make sure this sage advice has registered in her independent little mind. "And after that, if they decide they love each other so much that they want to spend the rest of their lives together, they get married."

Far from being the end of the matter, this explanation sparked a torrent of inquiry. "Why do they have to talk to their parents? How come they have to get married in front of everybody? Why do they want people to give them presents?"

I kept up as best I could, but wished, not for the first time, that my 6-year-old-going-on-20 could be content with childhood and its childish dreams. But Becky's sights have always been set on the prize just beyond her reach, so I've never had any choice but to prepare her to take hold of it.

After a few incompetent starts, her father and I have concluded that the best way to prepare our precocious daughter to take hold of this future love is to plunge her young roots deeply into the foundation of eternal love—the only foundation that can instill within her the unshakeable conviction that she is absolutely, unconditionally, irreversibly loved by us and by her God. A foundation with a built-in sense of value and identity in Christ that can't be compromised without her consent. A foundation upon which God can build the solid structure of a courageous, loving character.

And when it's time for her to take possession of this prize for which her young heart already yearns, we'll praise God as we present her, radiant and secure in Christ, capable of giving and receiving love, to the prince and the sunset of her choice—according to His will. (And after she talks it over with us.)

Sounds a little fatuous for our faded, sophisticated age? While it's true that mere humanistic optimism is a futile, impotent self-indulgence, the optimism and idealism that proceed from God are a different matter. They're made of different stuff. Our God encourages—even commands—us to hope and believe extravagantly, according to His "precious and magnificent promises," because He has the will and the power to back it all up (2 Peter 1:4, NASB).

So I don't apologize for cherishing the same extravagant, idealistic hopes for my church that I cherish for my romantic little girl. I insist on hoping and *believing* that this diverse body of believers will

113

not ultimately falter but will thrive and develop until it becomes "mature, attaining to the whole measure of the fullness of Christ" (Eph. 4:13, NIV). And I believe that when this happens, "when the character of Christ shall be perfectly reproduced in His people, then He will come to claim them as His own" (*Christ's Object Lessons,* p. 69).

I insist on believing this, not because *we* are worthy of such outrageous confidence, but because our Prince is faithful. He has determined to carry His beloved bride—His church—into a blissful, eternal sunset, and He will not fail.

But everything comes in its natural order. Before the total commitment of marriage can be appreciated or even desired, the foundation of emotional security and acceptance must be laid. Before the bride of Christ can blossom into full, radiant, spiritual maturity, the roots of the children must go down deep.

They must go deep into the solid, nourishing soil of God's *agape* love, a love that is, thankfully, not at all like the conditional, self-seeking love with which we're so familiar. It's a love that never says to its beloved, "Please me, and I'll accept you. Make it worth my while, and I'll stick around. Disappoint or inconvenience me, and I'll reject you."

In startling contrast to this fickle, self-centered human love, "God demonstrates His own love for us in this: While we were still sinners, Christ died for us" (Rom. 5:8, NIV). While we were still "dead in transgressions," God "made us alive with Christ" "because of His great love for us" (Eph. 2:4, 5, NIV).

This is an astonishing, unexpected love! While we were still our Father's disobedient children, unwilling to acknowledge His divine authority, incapable of comprehending or appreciating His infinite sacrifice, He loved us—He *saved* us! And with our consent, *this* is the love His indwelling Spirit will "shed abroad in our hearts"—the invincible *agape* love that constitutes the foundation for our new birth and childhood in Christ (Rom. 5:5, NIV).

An informed, intelligent appreciation of this love is the only antidote to our deep-seated, unconscious enmity and carnal distrust of God. It motivates us to tear our focus from ourselves and this world and place it squarely on Christ. Received into the heart, this love will create a holy environment in which spiritual and emotional security can flourish, enabling the children of God to grow up into the radiant bride of Christ, a spiritually mature companion fit for His divine company.

The self-absorbed Barbie can only dream of becoming such a bride—a bride who cares nothing for the exquisiteness of her gown or the whispered adulation of the guests. A bride who yearns only to be in the exquisite presence of her Beloved, to whisper her heartfelt adulation to Him, to unite her hopes and dreams with His for eternity.

This is the bride for whom Christ waits "with longing desire," with agonizing hopefulness (*Christ's Object Lessons,* p. 69). He waits and watches to see "the manifestation of Himself in His church"—in His bride—because He knows that her reception of His character of love constitutes her tacit consent to proceed with the wedding (p. 69). And no wedding can take place without the consent of the bride.

He calls to her now. He invites her to allow Him entry into the forgotten, subterranean chambers of her soul. "I stand at the door and knock," He pleads, "Open to me . . . my darling . . . my flawless one. My head is drenched with dew, my hair with the dampness of the night" (Rev. 3:20; Song of Songs 5:2, NIV).

The night is over. Eternity is breaking upon us. The consummation of the plan of salvation awaits our corporate commitment to receive and reflect "the last rays of merciful light, the last message of mercy to be given to the world—a revelation of [God's] character of love" (*Christ's Object Lessons,* p. 415).

# Teach Them to Your Children

Sabbath is a happy day," chirps the Sabbath school song, and for our family that's mostly true. Our kids are excited about their classes, love their teachers and friends, and bask in our family togetherness.

Even so, every Sabbath has its lag time. Incomprehensible sermons and marathon pew-warming sessions test our kids' goodwill to its limits, calling for massive amounts of parental patience and creativity. When this is missing, and we discourage our kids with outsized expectations of "appropriate behavior," Sabbath quickly deteriorates into a day they wish they'd never heard of. That's what happened to Jenny.

It all started on our way back to Sabbath school from a visit to the bathroom. As I skirted a huge puddle in the breezeway, I warned my daughter, "Watch out for the big puddle, honey." Sensing that my motherly advice had somehow been transposed in her 3-year-old mind to "Be sure to take a swim in the big, fun puddle, honey!" I turned, but too late. Eyes dilated with delight, Jenny was running straight for it. Before I could stop her, she skated into the center, lost her footing and flipped onto her side, shocked into breathless silence.

It didn't last long. Amazed at just how cold and deep a puddle can be, Jenny began howling her disapproval and pulling off socks and shoes with abandon. I dried her out as best I could, but the die was cast. Cold, and smarting from my thinly veiled irritation, Jenny quickly decided this was a bad Sabbath, and she was not going to like it.

Even when I grudgingly took her to the bathroom for the fourth time (her favorite diversion during long sermons) and ushered her into the favored "geen toy-it," she was not cheered. And after church, when Dad sharply terminated her mad gallop through the irresistibly empty sanctuary, her suspicions that all the world was against her were confirmed.

"Now I *know* Dad doesn't like me!" she sniffed through tired, frustrated tears.

I felt like shedding a few myself.

Sabbath is a happy day, as long as parents make it so. But when we burden our children with unrealistic expectations and harsh disapproval, it can be miserable and tear-jerkingly frustrating.

Christianity can be a happy experience too, when parents make it so. But when we clang our kids over the heads with burdensome rules and imperatives, obscuring its beauty and freedom, it's worse than a bad Sabbath. And because I'm temperamentally prone to burden and clang my little disciples all the way into the Promised Land, I pray often that the Lord will help me tread lightly into their fragile souls. I pray this because I take so seriously His admonition to "be careful, and watch yourselves closely so that you do not forget the things your eyes have seen or let them slip from your heart as long as you live. Teach them to your children and to their children after them" (Deut. 4:9, NIV).

I want so much to do just that. To introduce my children to their wonderful Saviour. To mold them into His loving, selfless image. To watch them grow and thrive throughout a safe and blissful eternity. I yearn to spare them the aching emptiness of a Christ-less childhood. Yet I realize that the very intensity of my desire makes it easy for me to pass the torch of Christianity with a heavy hand—and an iron will.

God has good news for parents like me. He tells us we don't need to drag our children into His presence, kicking and screaming. He has a better way, the way of love. "When we who are older become 'as little children,' when we learn the simplicity and gentleness and tender love of the Saviour, we shall not find it difficult to touch the hearts of the little ones and teach them love's ministry of healing" (*Adventist Home,* p. 195). Here is the Source of parental power to bring precious little ones to Christ. Here is a power greater and more effective than the intensity of the most focused human will— the attracting, transforming power of God's love, a love that will temper and soften the missionary zeal of the most devoted parent, yet empower us to appeal to the hearts and minds of our children.

Surrendered to this gentle, empathetic love of Jesus, we will again become as little children. We'll remember "how much [we] yearned for sympathy and love, and how unhappy [we] felt when censured and fretfully chided" (*Adventist Home,* p. 196). And we'll be mindful of the "different qualities of mind, . . . dispositions and temperaments," of our little ones, that we may "adapt [ourselves] to the work of patiently and kindly teaching [them] the way of the Lord" (*Child Guidance,* p. 207; *Adventist Home,* p. 183).

When I'm tempted to become exasperated with Jenny's frantic gymnastics during a Bible story, I'll remember her undeveloped attention span (and my own childhood wiggles). When I try to teach Becky to talk to Jesus "as to a friend," and she responds, "I don't *know* Jesus. How can He be my friend?" I'll seek to understand the extremely literal, concrete set of her mind (*Steps to Christ,* p. 93). And as I understand her better, I need not be scandalized when she sniffs, "I don't *want* to wear a white robe in the New Earth—I want to wear *pink!*"

So I watch and I pray and I strive to know these little bundles of intense individuality. I strive to understand and help them see their place in the body of Christ, the place He's designed just for them. I pray that "the truth as it is in Jesus" will be evident in me, that Christ may be real and comprehensible to them (*Christ's Object Lessons,* p. 129). I watch their "opening, receptive minds" taking it all in, catching a glimpse of the beauty and goodness of their Saviour, and my heart sings with joy (*Adventist Home,* p. 183).

When Becky surprises me by offering to pray and intercedes, "Dear Jesus, please keep Dad safe today, and please help Grandma and Grandpa to know You," I know I've witnessed a spiritual breakthrough.

When Jenny shyly whispers in my ear, "I asked Jesus to forgive me for talking mean to you this morning," I know that in spite of her endless fidgeting, my little one has been listening and learning. And when she sees the sun setting on Friday evening and shouts, "Oh, goody! It's Sabbath!" I'm thankful for another opportunity to learn to "call the Sabbath a delight" with my little girl (Isa. 58:13, NIV).

Even the Barbies bear witness to our kids' unfolding faith as they parade across the living room floor, decked out in their finest for Sabbath services at "Pastor Ken's" church, then submit to a bathtub baptism "in the name of the Father, and the Son, and the Holy Ghost—why do they say that, Mom?"

And so it goes, this remarkable journey into the land of Barbie baptisms and impromptu Sabbath swims, as I gather together the things my eyes have seen and my heart holds dear and teach them to my children. It's a grave and exalted and unpredictable privilege, heartwarming, unwittingly funny, frequently unsettling, as my children unexpectedly take on the role of teacher and expose my numerous deficiencies, sending me scrambling back to the sufficiency of my Saviour.

Don and I have found that it costs something to stand in the place of Christ to our children, to act as His delegated "ministers of grace." "It costs a mother's tears and a father's prayers" (*Child Guidance,* p. 479). It costs our precious adult egos with all their ridiculous baggage. It costs our souls' surrender to a loving Saviour.

But ours is the easy part, because the Lord is the One Who inspires our tears and prayers and makes them effective. He is the One Who paid so dearly to purchase our pitiful egos that we might receive His patience, kindness, and wisdom in their place. He is the One Who faithfully abides in us that His loving presence may win our children's open hearts to Him, for now and for eternity.

# Date Night

All the marriage and family literature recommends it. The lucky couples who have experienced it heartily endorse it. But wish as we might that we could join the ranks of those fortunate few, the hard truth remains—chronically broke and residing 30 long minutes from anywhere, the weekly date night eludes us. The monthly date night flees from us. But, pretty much by default, we've managed to nail down the semi-annual date night.

Every six months or so Don and I throw parental dignity to the wind and feverishly exclaim, "We can't take it anymore!" And notwithstanding our impoverished state, we entrust our precious girls to the care of a close friend or loving grandma and speed down Highway 93, desperately searching for that elusive commodity called "time alone."

Of late our dates have departed from their pleasant but unremarkable routine and have taken on an epic, ill-fated quality. Take my birthday last January. Don and I had planned to hike through the neighboring mountains, then drive to Kingman for dinner. But after the hike was rained out and our Chinese dinner was finished, we found ourselves all dressed up (for us) with no place to go. Home was out of the question. Our friend Vickie had offered to watch the kids until bedtime, and we didn't for an instant entertain the thought of returning a moment sooner.

So what to do? As we cruised through the rain-soaked streets of downtown Kingman, Don hit on a winning idea. Why not treat me to a driving tour of the local industrial park where he had spotted some especially intriguing scrap metal? Twenty minutes and many abandoned fuselages and freight cars later, Don sighed, "So what would you like to do now?"

I shook my head. "I don't know, honey. The industrial park is pretty hard to beat. How about a long, romantic drive around the county landfill?"

We laughed at ourselves and turned toward home, enjoying the quiet and each other's company. As the sun set behind an impenetrable curtain of clouds, we pulled off the highway for a romantic interlude before returning to family life as usual.

However, while some dates are destined for romantic greatness, this was not to be one of them. Our interlude was soon intruded upon by a faint but insistent scratching at my door. I sighed in disbelief. Scratching, banging, and other vexing noises at my door were what I had left home to escape. We tried to block it out, but it persisted, and was soon accompanied by a soft whimpering.

Surely the kids hadn't followed us here! I peered through my streaming window into the deepening dusk, straining to find the face of the mysterious, whimpering scratcher. My gaze fell on the graying muzzle of an ancient, brindle boxer, her mouth fixed in a desolate cry of woe, her emaciated body convulsed with cold. Her clouded brown eyes gazed into mine, pulsing out palpable waves of sorrow.

So much for romance. Wet as she was, Don and I loaded her into the car and hauled her home—but only until a permanent home could be found, we told each other. We soon regretted our hasty compassion.

Our dogs received her amiably, but she would have none of them. Our children tried to console her, but she rebuffed them. Spurning the shelter of the doghouse, she stood at our front door in the freezing rain, moaning pitifully to be allowed in, which my allergies would not permit. Day and night she watched me through the windows, her skeletal face following my every move, until I began to suffer from guilt overload. And when she attacked our beloved cat, Sam, I couldn't bear to have her around any longer. Much as we hated it, with nowhere else to take her, we reluctantly drove her to the pound.*

I was still pondering her fate when our next date rolled around. It had only been five months since our last date, but we made an exception for our anniversary. On a cloudless Sunday morning we waved goodbye to our daughters and Grandma Jeanne. Coaxing our balky Nissan over the craggy Black Mountains, we drifted down into the furnace heat of the Colorado River valley.

We had it all planned. We'd spend the day on the lake, the night in a hotel, and finish off with a hike in the mountains. And we would spare no expense. So we fantasized, until we reached the marina and got an eyeful of the watercraft prices: patio boats, $25 per hour; ski boats, $36 per hour. The jet-skis weren't even in the ballpark. We settled on the humble fishing boat. At $35 for four hours of thrills, it was a bargain.

We tossed our gear into the swaying aluminum hull, nudged old Number 10 out of her berth, and purred through the harbor into the open water of Lake Mohave. Then we turned on the power. Slicing through the choppy water at speeds approaching 10 miles per hour, the sun in our eyes and the wind in our hair, we drank in our unaccustomed freedom like a pair of truant teenagers. Who cared that our hands ached from gripping the greasy throttle, or that our teeth rattled from the vibrating outboard motor? We were together.

We spent the afternoon exploring, swimming, and resting in the quiet coves. In the evening we cruised back into the harbor, woozy from four hours of breathing gasoline fumes in the scorching heat. After a peaceful night's sleep in a bed I didn't make and a wonderful breakfast I didn't prepare, we left the sultry Colorado for the cool breezes of the Cerbats, the mountains behind our home. Up the winding, narrow road we jolted, crashing over rocks and executing hairpin turns a little faster than we would have liked. With no first gear (it had become history months before), we didn't dare slow down.

We parked at the trailhead and hiked toward the summit, drinking in the view and the soft whispering of the wind through the Ponderosa pines. Climbing above the tree line, we scrambled through the thorny scrub to the bald crown of Cherum's Peak, where we discovered the summer home of the ladybugs who had long since fled the desert heat. We sat silently for some time, admiring the circling hawks, feeling the wind tear at our hair and our clothes, contemplating the gray speck of a mobile home 3,000 feet below, that sheltered our two precious distractions.

"Well, is it time?" I finally asked.

My husband consulted his watch. "Yeah. I think it's time."

Rested, invigorated, fortified against another six months of parental combat duty, we descended the trail to our humble brown wagon. "Back to the real world," Don smiled, as he turned the key—which coaxed not one spark of life from our intractable vehicle. "Oh, no!" we groaned in unison, as we gazed longingly at our beckoning home, still 2,000 feet below and eight miles away.

Real world, indeed. Apparently we had never left it. It had followed us all the way to the mountain, once again intruding upon a well-scripted date. But we didn't really mind. We had already agreed that "two are better than one," because "if one falls down, his friend can help him up" (Eccl. 4:9, 10, NIV). And whether we fall down, bog down, or break down, my best friend and I would rather meet life's inevitable intrusions together than experience even the best that life has to offer alone. So we locked the car and headed down the mountain, glad for the pleasant weather and the comfort of one another's company.

---

*Good news, dog lovers—the boxer was later seen romping through a Kingman park with her loving, adoptive owner.

# Fowl Language

I've been accused of being easily entertained. The accusation is true, and I've decided to stop trying to live it down and just accept it as a compliment. I admit it—I'm an uncool, unsophisticated throwback to an earlier, more primitive culture. I have yet to be introduced to the mysteries of the Internet. I'd sigh with relief if I knew I never had to drag my weary body through another mega-priced, mega-hyped super mall. And the very thought of viewing the latest adrenaline-charged, high-tech video spectacle makes me want to bolt for the nearest exit.

I'd trade it all in a moment for a good, close brush with nature, not just at its most sublime, but at its most unassuming. Though I revel in the majesty of the mountains and the glories of a desert sunset, I thrive on the small and commonplace—a bustling ant hill with its busy troops toting tiny grains of decomposed granite out and tiny seeds and leaves in; a motley crowd of range cows lounging with their calves in the thin shade of a scrub oak, switching their skinny tails at summer flies.

Recently I spent many happy hours digging and constructing a worm composter—a two-by-four-foot, mulch-lined, plywood-covered hole in the ground for housing composting worms. When the UPS man arrived with my order of five hundred Red Wigglers, fresh from Uncle Jim's Worm Farm, I was as excited as my kids to watch the little guys devour their daily ration of banana peels and melon rinds.

But what I really enjoy is hanging out in the chicken yard—not by the hour, just for a few lingering moments after scattering their beloved scratch. I love to listen to their mellow, contented clucks and watch their bobbing heads bounce from side to side, then ratchet up and down when they've found some especially rich grazing. I chuckle at their enraged squeals and squawks as they vie for the same coveted speck of cracked corn.

It's true that chickens aren't the most intelligent domestic creatures, and certainly not the most devoted. They won't save you from a burning building or purr contentedly in your lap as you gaze languidly into a hearth full of glowing embers on a cold winter's night. They won't snuggle sympathetically at your side as you pour out your deepest secrets and darkest sorrows. But to a kid growing up in the distinctly fowl-free suburbs of southern California, chickens symbolized country—a place and a state of mind in which I yearned to live. And to my ears, a flock of contentedly clucking chickens still says "country," loudly and eloquently.

Our first chickens came to us during our first spring on the Tuckahoe, when some old friends thought our girls needed two banty chicks for Easter. Rosie and Grandma spent their first few days making a mess of the bathtub while I frantically figured out what to do with them. They graduated to a cardboard box while I penetrated the mysteries of poultry management in "A Guide to Raising Chickens." By the time they started flapping around the laundry room, I was ready to move them into their custom-built coop. As they strutted around their new home, scratching up pine shavings and cackling their approval, I knew I had arrived. Our humble desert homestead had been transformed into a real country home.

Our little flock has gone through a lot of changes since then. Poor Grandma fell prey to prowling coyotes, as did Mary and Theresa. Cute little Rosie grew up to become such a belligerent, obnoxious rooster that we shipped him off to our friend Sue's, along with the equally obnoxious Thelma and the flighty, paranoid Lucille. That's when we decided to swear off the high-strung, gallivanting banties and start fresh with the calmer, full-sized breeds. And that's how we ended up with Mary (the Second) and Laura and Grandma (the Second) and Cuddles.

Mary was an agreeable Rhode Island Red, Laura a cranky, but productive Barred Rock, and Grandma and Cuddles were identical white Delawares. We settled them into their new home, confident they'd be safe behind the sturdy, six-foot fence we'd just erected. Surely no coyote could penetrate this fortress. But we'd soon learn that the muddled inner workings of the chicken mind would render that unnnecesary.

One morning while I was showering, Becky shrieked, "Mom, a coyote—and he's got one of the chickens!"

By the time I rushed out to investigate, the white feathers fluttering to the ground told the sad tale. Apparently one of the Delawares had become so unnerved by the presence of a lurking coyote that she had flapped, panic-stricken, into the air, over the fence, and smack into his astonished jaws.

We felt bad about the poor hen, but we were in a quandary. We couldn't figure out which one was left. Jenny was certain it was Grandma (her hen), while Becky maintained it must be Cuddles (her hen). Lacking the wisdom and dramatic flair of Solomon, I didn't think to ask for a sword. So we settled on a workable compromise. We named the remaining hen Grandma Cuddles, and everyone was happy.

Still, our chicken yard was missing an essential element—that glorious greeting of the rising sun that only a rooster can provide. So back we went to Sue, who sent us home with Fluffy and Shadrach. Fluffy was a sweet little gray pullet (so we thought), who got along with everyone. Shadrach was a handsome yellow and green rooster, so-named because we'd snatched him from the jaws of Southern fried certain death. He was gentlemanly, even shy around the hens. And so they mingled together, passing their days happily, scratching and pecking.

But in the chicken yard, balance of power is a delicate thing. In time, our peaceful Shadrach turned into a bloodthirsty tyrant, surpassing Rosie for spite. And when Fluffy, who grew from a little gray "hen" into a big gray rooster, couldn't keep his claws off the irresistible hens, the proverbial feathers flew. They flew from dawn till dark, as the two rivals noisily squared off with a great show of dire wing-flapping and chest-puffing, and the hens squawked and flapped in alarm. Though we hated to do it, we realized that if peace were to return to the chicken yard, Shadrach must return to the fire from whence he was saved. Against his vigorous protests, we packed him into a cage while we tried to contact Sue. All day long we tried, without success. And all day long Shadrach fought that cage until his comb was bloody and bruised, and we feared he'd do himself in. We needn't have worried. Though we didn't know it yet, Shadrach was destined to escape the fire a second time. Even as he thrashed and sputtered, deliverance was on the way.

It arrived in the afternoon in the person of Max, who rumbled up with a flatbed full of steel for my husband. While Max wrestled channel iron off the truck, we chatted about the weather and the changing fortunes of the scrap metal industry. And the whole time, I kept thinking, *I wonder if I should ask this guy if he wants a rooster.* Often plagued by such fanciful thoughts, I'm used to squelching them before they leak out. *Of course you shouldn't ask him if he wants a rooster!* I shushed myself. *He'll think you're a complete fool!*

Then Max began to gush about his cherished country acreage, his goats, and his beloved flock of more than 20 hens, who were sorely in need of an unattached rooster to vex and otherwise complicate their lives. Which just goes to show, it takes one unsophisticated, chicken-loving fool to know one. Wrapped in the trappings of middle class civility, we still know who we are. And we know where to find the soul of the country—in the chicken yard, where the eggs are warm and fresh, the presence of measurable intelligence is questionable, and the soft, reassuring strains of fowl language are music to our ears.

# The Presence of God

Christmas. That time of year when covetousness is exalted to the status of art, if not religion. When Santa is commissioned to deliver the battery-operated heart's desire of every good boy and girl. And MasterCard is entrusted with the cravings of their parents. When warm, fuzzy sentimentalism drips from holiday programs like water from a leaky faucet. That time of year when sincere Christians blanch at the secularism and crass commercialism of it all and earnestly admonish one another to "keep Christ in Christmas this year."

Which forces a confession from my guilty lips: I don't know how to do it. I don't know how to keep Christ in Christmas. And not only do I not know how to "keep" Him there (and I say it respectfully), I have never known how to "put" Him there in the first place.

This is not to say I don't like Christmas. I enjoy

135

the beautiful carols, the festiveness, the customary feast. I cherish the fellowship with family and friends and feel especially satisfied when we can share ourselves and our home with those who have no family. But basically I experience Christmas as comforting cultural tradition, not sacred event. Earnest appeals of the Christian community notwithstanding, I am just not able to generate a seasonal sense of awe for the birth of my Saviour.

The Lord knows of my scandalously Scroogian incapacity. He knows I'm incapable of keeping Him close to me during Christmas, or any other time of year. That's why He's called Immanuel—God with us—because it's *His* job to come near and keep Himself close to me. As I raise my children and love my husband and relate to my church and my community, even in the hustle and glitz of the Christmas season, Jesus makes it *His* business to "keep *my* soul and deliver *me* . . . for I put my trust in [Him]" (Ps. 25:20).

And the wonderful thing is, even *before* I knew how to put my trust in Him, *before* I acknowledged Him as Lord of my life, Christ took the initiative in keeping Himself near and drawing me closer to Him. And if the Christmas season does little else for me, perhaps it can lend itself to a recounting of some of those times when, though unconverted, I was attentive enough to sense the presence of the One Who calls Himself "God with us."

Kelly Hall housed some of Boston's most difficult-to-manage developmentally disabled residents—and Peter Forte was undeniably its most "challenging" occupant. His destructive and bizarre behaviors continually frustrated my attempts to keep order among the five men in my care. But in spite of all this—or perhaps because of it—the end of my swing shift invariably found me sitting at Peter's bedside, holding his dry, bony hand, trying to soothe away the demons so this unfortunate man could rise to thrash his way through another monotonous day of institutionalization. At such unlikely times, in such disheartening service, I sensed the encouraging, compassionate presence of God.

Chronically ill children live a different reality than their sturdier peers. As a severely asthmatic child in smoggy southern California, I learned early that life was not all fun and games. I knew the consequences of a night of hide and seek in the damp coastal air. I knew the E.R. nurses at St. Francis Hospital by name. I knew what it meant to spend the night with my head propped on the dining room table, agonizing over every breath, waiting for the sun to rise and bring blessed relief. At such exhausting times, weak and oppressed, I sensed the empathetic, comforting presence of God.

October 1980, and I was hitchhiking on Washington's Highway 97. I was picked up by a man and his young son. Ignoring my unpromising exterior, Ron and David invited me to their house for some delicious, nourishing vegetarian fare. On the way there, Ron broke all the rules of Adventist witnessing and blurted, "Have you ever heard of Ellen G. White? We believe she's a prophet. I think you'd enjoy her books."

At that moment the hair on the back of my neck literally stood on end, and a silent, authoritative voice commanded, "Listen to this man. He's going to tell you something that will change your life." At that time, and others like it, I've experienced the spine-tingling, compelling presence of God.

I can only wonder at the undeserved affection of this great God, this Supreme Monarch of the universe, Who has so treasured my questionable company as to consistently take the initiative in identifying Himself with my daily concerns, my chronic illnesses, even my prodigal youth—long before I ever began to return the favor.

I can only marvel at the persistence of this Holy Spirit, Who has so lovingly hounded my steps and mercifully broken into my life at just the right times and in just the right ways, startling me from my habitual self-preoccupation, long before I appreciated it.

I can only be forever grateful for the condescension of this Saviour called Immanuel, "Who, being in very nature God . . . made himself nothing, and in all things chose to be made like unto his brethren. . . for the suffering of death—even [my] death on a cross!" (see Phil. 2:6, 7, NIV; Heb. 2:17, 9; Phil. 2:8, NIV).

Truly, I am not able to "put" or "keep" this mighty God anywhere. I can only prostrate myself in His holy, pervasive presence and allow Him entrance into my broken heart, that "God *with* us" may be permitted to live out His perfect, redemptive will as "Christ *in* [me], the hope of glory" (Col. 1:27).

# CHAPTER 23

# Nobody Knows the Trouble I've Seen

Some years outshine all others in cherished memory, blazing like beacons of hope and excellence, bathing us ever after in the warm glow of gratitude and satisfaction. The Year of the Unexpected Love. The Year of the Longed-for Child. The Year of Healing and Restoration.

Then there are those vile, ill-conceived years that slouch irritably from one evil inconvenience to the next, wreaking havoc as they go, making us wish we'd never made their perverse acquaintance. For our family, that year was 1997—The Year of the Subversive Car.

Our car's subversive behavior began promptly in January when, at the turn of the key, it made noises as if it *wanted* to start, as if, should we coax it just *one* more time, it would be too happy to oblige. It proved to be a ruse. We soon realized it had no intention of turning over, or even telling us why. Its computer shamelessly lied, supplying a bogus repair code. We had no choice but to let it languish in our driveway until April, when we could afford to tow it into town for treatment.

Sporting a new throttle position sensor (whatever that is), it served us, more or less faithfully, until camp meeting, when its ailing transmission decided to go south. Though we could no longer drive it on the highway, for a few more months we sweet-talked it through our daily visits to the Chloride post office. But when it began to sound more like a garbage disposal than a car, we parked it.

Parked and at peace, our little wagon languished again until after Christmas, when Don was able to complete the tiresome process of rebuilding its transmission. When the kids and I heard its familiar four-cylinder purr, we jumped for joy —until Don came in with the incredible news: there was no fourth gear. Somehow, as faithfully as he had followed the repair manual's instructions, the synchro-assembly between third and fourth gears had been installed backward, and fourth gear had become, for all practical purposes, extinct.

"What happens when you put it in fourth?" I asked.

"Nothing," he replied, in his enigmatic way.

"Oh. So you'll be fixing that soon?" I asked, hopefully.

"Not for a while. We'll just have to get used

to driving it this way until I have time to take it apart again."

If only this was the whole of it. My first trip back from Kingman revealed that not only had fourth gear flown the coop, third gear had taken over. Even when it *appeared* to let me downshift smoothly into second, it never allowed second to engage; and it didn't even make a pretense of letting me shift up to fifth. Certain I'd be stranded 20 miles from home with a car full of perishables and two wiggly children, I snarled and slammed the stick shift around until I couldn't get it into *any* gear, and my kids asked in alarm, "What's wrong with the car, Mommy?"

"Oh, nothing that 30 seconds with a car crusher wouldn't fix," I hissed through clenched teeth. When we finally limped up the driveway, I hotly informed my husband that I would "never drive that piece of garbage again" until it was *really* fixed.

He calmly replied, "You just don't understand what's taking place in the transmission." He had that right. "What you need to do is shift into fourth before you try to put it in fifth, and even before you downshift into second."

This was not only irrational, it was beginning to sound like an Abbot and Costello routine. "Why should I put it in fourth when it doesn't *do* anything—and why should I shift into fourth before downshifting to *second?*" I protested.

"Because that will take it out of third and put it into neutral so you *can* shift to second," he reasoned, as though even a child could understand such convoluted logic.

My solution was to swear off the car as long as I could get away with it—until my children complained, "Mommy, there's no more food in the cupboards," and I had no choice but to make that long drive back to Kingman.

Now, if even *this* was the worst of it, 1997 might have been salvageable. We could (possibly) have laughed at the absurdity of it all and gone on with life. But add to it Don's multiple work-related injuries, his ancient pickup's perpetual breakdowns, and our implacable debt, and by the end of the year we felt like moaning the old spiritual, "Nobody knows the trouble I've seen; nobody knows but Jesus."

Except we often forgot to moan that last part. We so easily forgot that Jesus knew and cared deeply about every shred of trouble we'd seen in that long, treacherous year. And even when we did remember that He knew and cared and were comforted by the thought, we hesitated to take that next step—to say with any conviction, "We also *rejoice* in our sufferings, because we know that suffering produces perseverance, perseverance character, and character hope (Rom. 5:3, 4, NIV).

Now, I don't know about you hardcore stoics out

143

there, but at our house "rejoice" and "suffering" are two words we've never been tempted to even whisper in the same breath. In fact, we have a strong natural aversion to finding ourselves uncomfortably wedged between these strange bedfellows. But to the extent that we've resisted the urge to struggle against them and have even grudgingly regarded our recent difficulties as teachers instead of executioners, we've learned some surprising lessons.

We've learned that, although "it is more blessed to give than to receive," it's also no shame to receive when you're in need (Acts 20:35). Don and I are hardworking, self-sufficient people. Too self-sufficient. We've always felt far more comfortable extending the hand that gives, rather than the hand that receives. But when a thoughtful, attentive member of our church family noticed our chronic transportation woes and insisted on helping with a generous gift, we decided to gratefully accept. Which is why our car, such as it is, runs at all.

And when some other brothers and sisters realized we couldn't afford a Christmas tree for our kids (or much else, including new tennis shoes to replace my tattered ones), they quietly prevailed upon us to accept some assistance and saw to it that we got a living pine tree. Now every time I lace up my tennies, and every time we admire that island of living green in our desert landscape, we remember the kindness of the family of God. And we thank Him for their gifts of love in our time of need.

We've also begun to rediscover the lost art of being content. We're not sure when or how we lost this capacity, but somewhere along the way it seemed to take more money, more "freedom," and more control to make us feel that our life was worth living. Somewhere along the way, we bought into the belief that success and prosperity were our sovereign right. We've found that a good dose of helplessness has a way of turning such thinking on its arrogant little head.

I think it was in October that I really began to resent being stranded on this remote piece of desert with two young children, no car, no money, and no close friends. People shook their heads and marveled at how I put up with such incredible deprivation. Indeed, I complained (often) to Don that I felt trapped, nailed to the ground.

And then an astonishing thing happened. I began to enjoy it. I began to enjoy the freedom of getting up in the morning and having no place to go. Strangely, I began to enjoy the freedom of having no money to spend and nowhere to spend it. I began to really cherish (and not just put up with) my children's company. And I became grateful that the Lord doesn't spoil us by giving us what we think we want. He loves us enough to painstakingly show us and grant us the true "desires of [our] hearts" (Ps. 37:4).

Our troubles have reminded us that God didn't adopt us into His family to grant us immunity from the hardship and heartache that characterize so much of the human experience. Though our Heavenly Father is able to spare His children much of the destruction that the unconverted mind brings upon itself, it's not His intention to create of us a pampered, privileged class. It's His plan to generate from our common affliction a healing empathy that reaches beyond our pain to minister to our fellow sufferers.

We've also become convinced that God can be trusted far more than we ever cared to find out. He can be trusted not only to know and care about our trials, but to unobtrusively slip into our lives to help and heal and provide at just the right time. A pickup load of scrap wire and aluminum just when we wondered how we'd buy the groceries. A call from a trusted friend to lift us above the isolating anxiety into which we'd sunk.

And when, in spite of all our exhausting work and anxious prayers, we saw no evidence that our needs would be met at all, we were sustained by God's promises to provide. And we were encouraged by the record of His care for His church in the desert. " 'The children of Israel did eat manna forty years . . . until they came unto the borders of the land of Canaan. For forty years they were daily reminded by this miraculous provision of God's unfailing care and tender love. . . . Sustained by 'the corn of heaven,' they were daily taught that, having God's promise, they were as secure from want as if surrounded by fields of waving grain on the fertile plains of Canaan" (*Patriarchs and Prophets, p. 297*).

Most of all, we've been impressed that the quality of our trust in God and our reasons for trusting Him affect much more than our own peace of mind and quality of life, or even our spiritual security. They make a public statement about our Lord and about why He is worthy to be served. To the extent that our trust does not persevere under trial, we agree with Satan: "Does Job fear God for nothing?" "You have always protected him and his home and his property from all harm. You have prospered everything he does—look how rich he is! No wonder he 'worships' you! But just take away his wealth, and you'll see him curse you to your face!" (Job 1:9, NIV; 1:10, 11, TLB).

To the extent that trust perseveres and Christ's character is formed within us, we are privileged to know God at a level of deep devotion that transcends our carnal desire to live a charmed, exempted life. To the extent that our devotion to God is cleansed of the unconverted obsession with material and spiritual security, we can rise with Job "to the heights of implicit trust in the mercy and the saving power of God," and say before the watching universe, "Though he slay me, yet will I trust in him" (*Prophets and Kings,* p. 163; Job 13:15).

As we wrestled with the difficult events of 1997 and those we've encountered since, we've sensed the Lord whispering an insistent question, the same question He asked the prophet Jeremiah, who faced far more severe hardship and perplexity than we've ever known: "If you have raced with men on foot and they have worn you out, how can you compete with horses? If you stumble in safe country, how will you manage in the thickets by the Jordan?" (Jer. 12:5, NIV).

As people preparing for the coming of our Lord, we ask ourselves, If we become offended and discouraged by mere inconvenience, or even real, but tolerable hardship, how will our Christianity fare when faced with severe deprivation and persecution? And if we're continually "ready to faint at every obstacle" we encounter on our way to the Promised Land, how can we honor our Lord when we arrive at its very border and confront that final, cataclysmic tribulation, "such as the world has never before seen in all its history, and will never see again" (*Patriarchs and Prophets,* p. 292; Matt. 24:21, TLB)?

There is only one answer—Job's answer: "My ears had heard of you but now my eyes have seen you. Therefore I despise myself and repent in dust and ashes" (Job 42:5, 6, NIV). If we have merely "heard" of God, knowing Him only vaguely and theoretically, there is no hope for us at the end of all things, or even now, while we abide in relatively "safe country." Our only hope is in learning to *see* God—firsthand, experientially, intimately.

When vehicles leave us stranded in the middle of nowhere, when injury or illness come home to stay, when hopes and plans are abruptly derailed and there are none to take their place, we can practice the spiritual discipline of discerning Christ at the center of the storm, clinging to us with the ferocious tenacity of a devoted mother clinging to her weak, endangered child. Accepting our utter helplessness, and resisting the urge to tear ourselves from His determined, capable grasp, we will endure all manner of tribulation—and show the world that ours is a "great God, mighty and awesome," able to save "to the uttermost" all who place their trust in Him (Deut. 10:17, NIV; Heb. 7:25).

# Hungry for Love

One Sabbath afternoon last summer a visitor came calling at our gate. Thank the Lord the gate was closed or our pushy visitor no doubt would have slithered right into our yard and, possibly, on through our open front door, into the cool shadows of our living room. As it was, all he could do was coil into a venomous heap, rattle out an anxious alarm, and strike helplessly at the welded wire that stood between him and our furiously barking dog, Bo.

"Rattlesnake!" screamed our terrified daughters as they fled from their swing set into the house.

My husband leapt to the rescue, and after a few quick thrusts with a well-aimed shovel, the snake was history. We buried his head and tossed his still-undulating carcass into the brush beyond the house. Twenty-four hours later, the carcass was gone. The sometime predator had traveled full circle to become the prey.

The desert is a hungry place. It tolerates no neutrality in the grand, desperate scramble for survival. One must hunt or be hunted, eat or be eaten—or run fast enough to earn another breath and heartbeat. The restless screech owls, hawks, and coyotes are sustained, though never fattened, by the elusive lizards, cottontails, and kangaroo rats. The rattlesnakes settle for what they can get and, in turn, sometimes succumb to a brazen roadrunner. And the hunger hasn't stopped at our gate, as our loss of five chickens and two dogs testifies.

The human soul is a hungry place. It is driven, at its core, by a deep, wordless craving for love and truth, for fellowship and purpose. The Lord, in His goodness, has placed the hunger there, and He is the only One who can satisfy it. But when His loving overtures are repeatedly spurned or misunderstood, the hunger goes awry, and life becomes a base, desperate struggle for survival of self.

Caught up in this struggle, we learn to play out the complex, interdependent roles of predator and prey. We learn when to dominate and when to submit. We become adept at deriving life through the diminishing of another. We are manipulated and exploited and feel ourselves painfully diminished. And if this cycle of destructive hunger is not allowed to be divinely interrupted, it is delivered as a legacy from one generation to the next.

Such has been the case with our families. My

husband and I received this legacy of hunger from our parents, who received it from their parents before them. And as did they, we sought fulfillment, or at least relief, through the destructive avenues of the world—appetite and sensuality, alcoholism and workaholism, materialism, drug abuse, and the occult. Avenues that had become entrenched in the family genes and psyche. Avenues that prey upon the innocent and unsuspecting and teach them, in turn, to practice the unloving ways of the predator.

When we became Christians, Don and I turned our backs on this cycle of sin. We had found the Desire of our hearts, and we thought our soul hunger would now be satisfied. But our initiation into parenthood made it painfully clear that we had underestimated the imprint of our family legacy and overestimated the depth of our conversion.

To our shame, we have often behaved not as loving parents, but as rivals toward our children. Because we have not known enough of real love, we've competed with them for that precious commodity and diminished them in the process. We've yearned to do otherwise—to nurture our daughters lavishly, with no thought for ourselves. But our own unsatisfied soul hunger has compelled us to grasp greedily and dispense grudgingly the love that always seemed to be in such limited supply.

The Lord is showing us a way of escape from our legacy of gnawing hunger and its attendant cycle of sin—the way of corporate repentance. He's helping us to see that in order to be fully freed from the past our repentance must be large and generous enough to comprehend, by faith, the entire body of sin to which we have become heir. Not merely sin that we have personally practiced and cherished, but "family" sin that we shrink from in disgust. Absent the restraining influence of the Holy Spirit, that sin is ours.

"*I* could never do such a thing!" is gradually being replaced with "I am no better than my ancestors" (1 Kings 19:4, NIV). And with that heartfelt admission has come an unprecedented freedom from the counterproductive "right" to blame, the paralyzing sense of victimization, the destructive anger, the compulsion to overcompensate. We are being set free from the old identity of predator and prey and becoming the blessed recipients of a new, eternal family identity in Christ—"partakers of the divine nature" (2 Peter 1:4, NIV).

We are partakers of the nature of a heavenly Father who declares, "I have loved you with an everlasting love; I have drawn you with lovingkindness" (Jer. 31:3, NIV). Partakers of the nature of a heavenly "Mother" who assures, "Can a mother forget the baby at her breast and have no compassion on the child she has borne? Though she may forget, I will not forget you! See, I have engraved you on the palms of my hands" (Isa. 49:15, NIV).

Released from our compulsion to repeat or react against the past, we're free to drink deeply of this divine parental love, and our deepest soul hunger is being satisfied. Transformed by this love, we're gradually becoming the divinely inspired parents our children need—parents who can help set them free from their own unique collection of "hereditary tendencies to evil" and establish in their generation a new family legacy of everlasting, soul-satisfying love (*Adventist Home,* pp. 172-174).

# CHAPTER 25

# All the Way Home

Anyone who has ever undertaken the risky business of clipping a wriggling child's nails knows the value of a good diversion. I always use the old standby (with certain vegetarian substitutions):

This little piggy went to market,
This little piggy stayed home.
This little piggy had tofu,
This little piggy had none.

And this little piggy went *wee, wee, wee,* all the way home!

Whenever my children tire of piggies, I vary the routine with the creature of their choice. Their wild and woolly fingers have been tamed to the tune of doggies, chickens, and Percy, the fire-belly newt, woofing, clucking, and swimming all the way to their respective homes.

In the days before I had children with wiggly fingers to tame, I hiked, biked, and even boated all the way to a wide assortment of homes, many of them decrepit and inconvenient structures for which the word "home" was really a generous euphemism. Homes with a bathroom "down the hall" that felt as though it was located in another county. Frigid homes in which the temperature in my basement bedroom plunged nightly to sub-zero levels. Crowded homes that I shared with throngs of creeping, scampering, non-human occupants.

One of my more memorable abodes was an ancient miner's shack—my "little hovel," as my father affectionately called it. "Hey, Les," he'd deadpan. "Sent that picture in to *Better Homes and Hovels* yet? They're begging to hear from you!"

OK, so it wasn't exactly uptown. The shower on the porch wasn't functional. The rusty tank hanging above it dispensed spiders, not water. There wasn't any water to dispense. I was thankful there was an outhouse—until that big storm blew away two of its walls on the side that faced my only neighbor.

The Okanogan Valley migrant worker's cabin had running water and a real bathroom just half a block away, along with an ample supply of flies wafting on the pungent breeze from the upwind corral.

The island off the Maine coast had running water, but no electricity. We didn't mind. The lamplit evenings were breathtaking.

And then there were the occasional homes— the YMCAs, the Salvation Army dormitories, the fields and woods where I camped while hitchhiking. Oh, yes, and the teepee.

For a time, all this home-hopping was great fun. Ablaze with the romance and restlessness of youth, I regarded it as the grand, transcontinental adventure of a lifetime. But a few years down the road, all the interstates began to look alike. Portland, Oregon, felt strangely similar to Portland, Maine. And I still hadn't managed to stumble across Paradise.

One winter evening in a Boston suburb, in a mood as dark and cold as the night, I withdrew from a group of friends and wandered alone beside a deserted railroad track. Suddenly overwhelmed by my rootlessness, I burst out, surprising myself, "Oh, God, I want to know You! I just want to know You."

At the time, I couldn't comprehend that the Lord Himself had filled me with that aching desire, had constrained me to speak those words. I didn't know that He had placed within me a homesickness for my eternal home with Him, the home He had already prepared for me in Christ.

But old habits die hard. For two more years I crisscrossed the continent. The Lord was undeterred, and patiently led me through an acute awareness of my loneliness into a deepening conviction of my sinfulness. And when I was willing, He led me into the arms of my Saviour and into fellowship with my new family, the Seventh-day Adventist Church.

Since then God has blessed me with my wonderful husband, our two beautiful daughters, and a home of our own—a home that, admittedly, has fallen into some neglect since I gave up being a compulsive housekeeper to become a compulsive writer. The grape juice that plasticized under the crisper last year is still there, lushly landscaped by an intriguing collection of dead bugs and pieces of things that used to be edible. The toaster crumbs have multiplied and compacted until they nearly set off the smoke alarm when we make toast.

And then there's the basket of Christmas nuts that vibrated off the back of the washer and rolled onto the floor between the washer and the wall. I told my husband, "They'll just have to stay there until I finish the book." And then I joked, "Maybe the mouse will cart them away first." The funny part is, he did. And I suppose it wasn't very kind of me to repay him by knocking him cold with the broom handle, when he only had one walnut left to go. .

But now the all-consuming book is finished, and our home can return to normal. The cat can stop glaring at me for hogging his cushy desk chair. The kids can stop crying, "Mom, quit writing and make us lunch! We're starving!" I can go to sleep, once again, at a reasonable hour and feel like a human being in the morning.

It'll be nice to get back to normal. But I'll miss my daily visits to the computer to share the events of our home and the thoughts of our hearts. And I'll miss sharing our hope of an eternity together "in peaceful dwelling places, in secure homes, in undisturbed places of rest" (Isa. 32:18, NIV).

Thank God, we have this common hope. When the cares and distractions of our earthly homes absorb us so that we can't see beyond them, and our heavenly home seems so far away, He reminds us that it doesn't need to be so. Heaven is as near as Christ. "As through Jesus we enter into rest, heaven begins here. We respond to His invitation, Come, learn of Me, and in thus coming we begin the life eternal. Heaven is a ceaseless approaching to God through Christ" (*Desire of Ages,* p. 331).

I pray that my church, my family, and I will have attentive hearts that can discern the presence of our loving Saviour, receptive hearts that can appreciate His eternal sacrifice in our behalf, submissive hearts that will follow Him as He leads us through this life—all the way home.